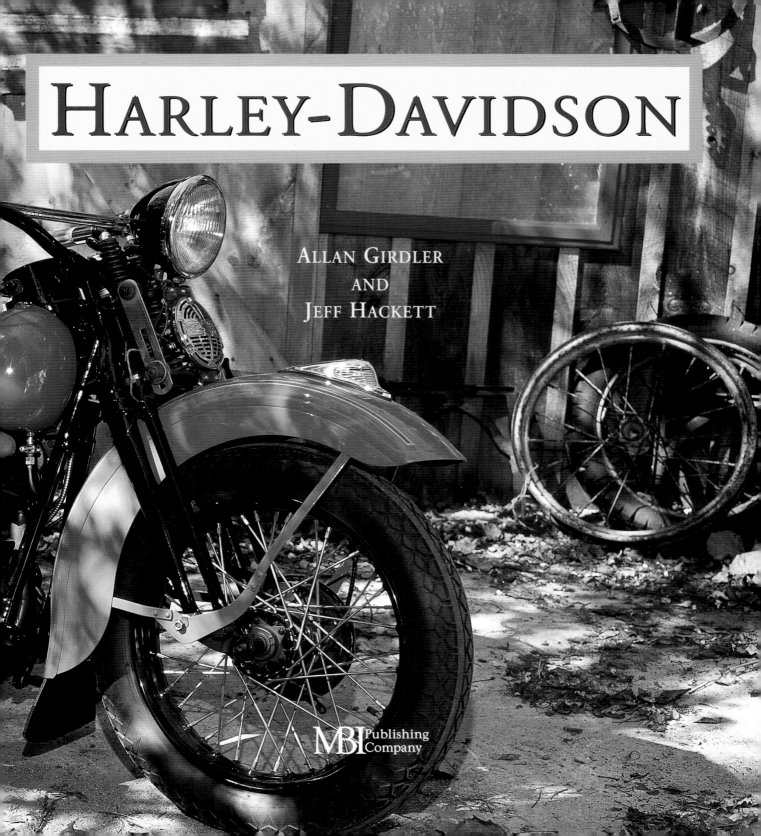

HARLEY-DAVIDSON

ALLAN GIRDLER

AND

JEFF HACKETT

MBI Publishing Company

Photographer Jeff Hackett would like to thank the following people for supplying the bikes used in this book: Barry Algreo (p. 30), Sly Barnes (p. 83), Benjy's H-D, Huntington, West Virginia (p. 65), Jeff Bergan (p. 60), Bob Bishop (pp. 38, 42), Dean Bordigioni, Golden Gate H-D (p. 86), Don Chateen (p. 70), Pat Conroy (p. 69), Jeffrey Culver (p. 82), Nancy Delgado (p. 79), Brent Dugan (pp. 50, 52), Bill Eggers (pp. 12, 15, 17), Pat Esposito (p. 43), Jason Fletcher/Fasthog Racing (p. 76), Lee Floren (pp. 72, 73), Dr. L. Friedman (p. 24), Carl Fronk (p. 92), Dave Fusiak (p. 34), Jerri Grindle (p. 75), Maureen Hansen (pp. 66, 68), Harley-Davidson Motor Co. (pp. 88, 93, 94, 95), David Janiszewski (pp. 28, 35), Dave Kiesow, Illinois H-D, Berwyn, Illinois (p. 33), Michael Lange (p. 22), Leon (p. 87), Woody Leone Sr. (p. 31), Bruce Linsday (p. 18), Dick Lloyd (pp. 84, 85), Tom Mahar (p. 61), Chris Maida, American Iron Mag., H-D Motor Co. (pp. 90, 91), Brendan Mier (p. 59), Raymond Miller (pp. 32, 37), Dave Minerva (pp. 1, 22, 23), Kyle Mussman (p. 21), Rick Newman (pp. 56, 62, 63), Vinny Pacifico (p. 86), David Paryzek (p. 53), Al Perry (p. 43), Mike Ruffino (p. 58), Dave Sarafan (p. 44, 45), Fred Schaub (p. 24), Roy Schneider (p. 42), Tom Sephton (p. 55), JD Russell Smith (p. 25), Ron Smith (p. 82), Mark Spencer, Spencer Cycle Shop, Belleville, New Jersey (p. 78), Ted Tine, Essex Motorsports, Essex, Connecticut (p. 26), Ray Turski (p. 68), Jim Wick (pp. 70, 71).

First published in 2000 by MBI Publishing Company, 729 Prospect Avenue, PO Box 1, Osceola, WI 54020-0001 USA

© Allan Girdler and Jeff Hackett, 2000

The information in this book is true and complete to the best of our knowledge. All recommendations are made without any guarantee on the part of the author or Publisher, who also disclaim any liability incurred in connection with the use of this data or specific details.

We recognize that some words, model names and designations, for example, mentioned herein are the property of the trademark holder. We use them for identification purposes only. This is not an official publication.

MBI Publishing Company books are also available at discounts in bulk quantity for industrial or sales-promotional use. For details write to Special Sales Manager at Motorbooks International Wholesalers & Distributors, 729 Prospect Avenue, PO Box 1, Osceola, WI 54020-0001 USA.

Library of Congress Cataloging-in-Publication Data

Girdler, Allan
        Harley-Davidson/Allan Girdler and Jeff Hackett
            p. cm.— (Enthusiast Color Series)
        Includes index.
        ISBN 0-7603-0799-7 (pbk. : alk. paper)
        1. Harley-Davidson Motorcycle—History.
        I. Hackett, Jeff II. Title III. Series
TL448.H3 G543 2000   2000
629.227'5—dc21   99-057009

On the front cover: The 1936 Knucklehead is perhaps the penultimate Harley; prized by collectors and the template for the Harley-Davidsons of the following 90 years. *Jeff Hackett*

On the frontispiece: Flawless restorations are wonderful things to see, but they are ultimately someone's interpretation of an original. This time-worn 1951 FL appears in original condition, a beauty that enthusiasts love to behold. *Jeff Hackett*

On the title page: The 1937 Knucklehead showcases Harley-Davidson's flair for timeless design and engineering. *Jeff Hackett*

On the back cover: Harley-Davidson has integrated the styling genius of old with the engineering prowess of today to create the Twin Cam 88-powered 2000 Deuce. *Jeff Hackett*

Edited by Lee Klancher
Designed by Tom Heffron

Printed in China

CONTENTS

INTRODUCTION

My hobby is vintage racing, my mount is a 1970 Harley-Davidson XR-750 (details in chapter 8 but don't go there yet), and my transportation from home to track and back is a pickup truck.

At every other gas stop, or so it seems, I'll be pumping and somebody, employee or customer, will notice the bike and the labels and ask, "Harley-Davidson? When did Harley get into racing?"

"Oh," I say in as polite a tone as I can muster, "about 1908."

True fact, as we'll see in chapter 2.

Harley-Davidson, the brand, the product, and the legend, is known and admired around the world. Kids of all ages and nationalities wave if a Harley is in motion and stop to talk if it's not. (In case any Norwegian, Danish, Swedish, or Finnish moms wonder who taught their kids to say "Harley-Davidson is Number One" in English, it was me, riding an FLH to North Cape, Europe's northernmost landfall.) However, just because nearly everybody knows the name and the badge and the motorcycle doesn't mean they know the history.

It's a history worth knowing because the facts reinforce the legend: Four men with little more than grit and talent founded a company that rules its field nearly a century later. Its current success was wrested from near disaster; the product is—what the founders intended—as good a value for the money as can be found in our current culture; and in today's throwaway economy what you get now is a whole lot like what your father and his father got years ago.

Harley-Davidson history is a collection of stories, capturing the changing times. There are enough technical innovations to delight the world's motorheads, while at the same time there are people, make that heroes and heroines, who would make even Hollywood or the History Channel stop and take notice.

This is a short, concise history. Not all the facts or models are included here nor are they supposed to be. Instead, this is a history of the highlights, done so the reader will know why and how Harley-Davidson became the icon it is today.

—Allan Girdler

Author Allan Girdler (no shades) with a group of Americans at the FIM International Rally at Epernay, France in 1999. That's Allan's trusty XR-750 painted with a flag in the foreground. *Eric Corlay*

CHAPTER 1

WORKING ON THE RAILROAD

1 9 0 3

Now that Harley-Davidson is a world-class success story, an American icon, and the only survivor of motorcycling's pioneering past, now that we can afford the luxury of hindsight, it's safe to ask an unsettling question: Did The Motor Company, as the folks at H-D headquarters refer to the firm, become the one American motorcycle maker that lived while 200-plus rivals died because Harley's founders were machinists and toolmakers rather than bicycle guys?

Although this machine was assembled years after H-D went into business, for display it is labeled 1903 and 1904 because it has parts from both those years. Unlike most motorcycles of the time, this bike was assembled starting with the engine, which was fitted to the center of the oversized frame, with the bicycle pedals added on. Next, the wheels were fixed solidly in the frame, front and back. And if you look really closely, you'll see that the lever controlling the tension of the drive belt against the pulleys is linked to a pedal that does the same thing. There were times riders needed both hands on the grips and times when they needed both feet on the ground, so this preclutch control gave riders a choice. *Courtesy Harley-Davidson Archives*

Let's start at the beginning. The inventors of the motorcycle were two men who were working independently around 1868 or maybe 1869. One was an American named Sylvester Roper who lived near Boston. The other was a French inventor, Louis Perreaux, who put a steam engine aboard a pedal-powered bicycle, just then patented in 1868 by Pierre and Earnest Michaux. Roper didn't bother with pedals or patents or with keeping records, but both machines worked, or so the sketchy records claim, but neither the world, the bicycle, nor steam power was advanced enough to allow for a second act.

Fifteen or so years later, after Otto Daimler built a sort-of motorcycle as a mobile test bed for his internal combustion engine, the world was infatuated with the safety bicycle, with pedals, and pneumatic tires. Bicycle racing was a major sport, and somebody built a lumbering device with an engine, two wheels, and a windbreaker, to be ridden in front of bicycles so the riders wouldn't have to fight the air. (Yes, they were drafting 70 years before the stock-car crowd invented the art.) Meanwhile, scores of bright and ambitious chaps saw how logical it was to mount a gas engine on a bicycle, and many of these individuals went into the motorcycle business. Indian, the best of that breed, was the joint product of an engineering genius, the first man to make a reliable pacer (as the draft-breakers were called), and a champion bicycle racer who already owned a thriving bicycle factory.

At the same time, in Milwaukee, Wisconsin, there were three brothers, Arthur, William, and Walter Davidson. Milwaukee was a railroad town, and the brothers were members of the skilled craftsman class: Arthur was a pattern maker, William a toolmaker and fabricator, and Walter an apprentice machinist.

Arthur and his pal William Harley, who worked as a fitter in a bicycle plant, were bicycle enthusiasts, using them for transportation and hunting and fishing expeditions. It seemed logical to them that a bicycle with a motor would get them farther, faster.

Both young men had mechanical aptitude and they had friends who could help, including one named Ole Evinrude (yes, *that* Evinrude), so they began studying and then building single-cylinder engines that could be bolted to a bicycle, or so they hoped.

Besides having a keen interest and aptitude for things mechanical, Harley and the Davidsons had something else in their favor—they were railroad guys. People form lifelong habits and impressions from where they first work. They adopt the culture around them. The railroad culture, back then especially, centered around the work ethic. The train had to get there. On time. Intact. Railroads weren't sport; they were real life.

The founders, seen here in an official photo from 1910. From the left, William A. Davidson, the older brother who ran the plant; Walter Davidson, natural rider and company president; Arthur Davidson, salesman and organizer; and William Harley, the chief engineer. As the poses and suits indicate, by this time the founders were grown men and owners of a successful business. *Courtesy Harley-Davidson Archives*

With a strong work ethic ingrained in them, around 1900 or 1901, Harley and Arthur Davidson began building engines and testing them. In 1902, or so legend claims, Walter was literally beneath a locomotive on the Missouri, Kansas and Texas Railroad in Parsons, Kansas, when he got a message inviting him to come home and ride the motorized bicycle brother Arthur and friend Harley had been building. (Not to spoil the story, but he also was heading for Milwaukee to attend brother William's wedding.)

What he found when he got there was a complete set of motorcycle parts rather than a motorcycle, and the deal was he could ride it when he had put it together. (He did, but not then and there, because the first motorcycle Harley and the Davidsons completed didn't actually run until the spring of 1903.)

Here's where the railroad training began to pay off. The engine ran well enough and long enough to make clear to them the inadequacy of the bicycle-scale frame the builders were using. So they went, as the cliché puts it, back to the drawing board. They made a larger engine, which would produce not only more power but would do so with less stress.

And they made a new frame, larger and with stronger (and heavier) tubing. Not only that, they placed the engine in the middle and looped the frame around and below the engine. If you look at the other pioneers from the turn of the century, you'll see bicycles, with the pedal and crank in the center and the engine added.

Hell for stout, as the saying goes. Beyond that the prototype motorcycle was as basic as could be. The wheels were solidly mounted in the frame and the

WILLIAM HARLEY, CHIEF ENGINEER

Serendipity may have played a part, but the major factor in H-D's early success was William Harley. On the one hand, Harley stepped out of the limelight. It was the Davidson brothers, three to one, who voted to call the infant manufacturing operation Harley-Davidson, on the grounds that it sounded better. (Davidson-Harley works as well as, oh, Royce-Rolls or Johnson-Ivor, eh?)

On the other hand, Harley did not hide his natural mechanical ability. He had enough to know he didn't know what he needed to know, so later, in 1903, when he was 23 years old and a grown man gainfully employed, Harley enrolled in the engineering school at the University of Wisconsin at Madison.

To appreciate this, move back a century. Only a tiny fraction of the population went to college then. Harley wasn't well-to-do, nor was his family. He worked his way through, waiting tables for a fraternity as well as doing after-school mechanical projects for firms near the school.

Commitment is the word that fits here. To top it off, while working his way through school, Harley provided Arthur Davidson (who was home in the family's back yard building two more motorcycles to order) with engineering and other practical advice.

In his senior year, when the partners and the industry knew the solidly mounted front wheels were fine on bicycles but not with engines added, Harley designed a front suspension—leading links controlled by coil springs—that not only was the best in the field at the time, but was good enough to serve for the next 40 years (and it would even later come back as the nostalgic Springer version of the Softail). The leading-link design was also licensed out for use by European factories.

Harley wasn't an innovator or a creative genius. Rather, he made sure something worked before it was adopted and that the product was good value even if it wasn't flashy. He viewed his work as being for the long run, and the company's long run is in large part due to the tradition he established.

forks. There was one speed, well, perhaps it's more accurate to say drive was direct, with a leather belt between the engine pulley and the rear wheel pulley, with a lever the rider moved to tighten or loosen the belt's grip. There were no lights or any road equipment as we know it now. To start, the rider pedaled up to speed, set the controls for the carburetor (the design of which had occupied a lot of Harley's time and drew on Evinrude's advice), and pulled the belt tight enough to turn the engine. When things went right, the engine ran and the pedals served as footrests.

What mattered in the motorcycling world of 1903 was that the prototype worked. Harley and the Davidsons knew how to make a motorcycle.

What came next is a matter of minor debate. Some accounts hold that the original idea was simply for William Harley and Arthur Davidson to build a motorcycle for their own use and that the business began when other people saw the prototype, knew it was a superior machine, and wanted one like it.

The other version, which seems more likely based on the time and money the pals put into the project, was that at some point between the first drawings and the first ride, they realized they could compete. This was an age of opportunity, so they took it one step at a time, and the Harley-Davidson Motor Company was born.

CHAPTER 2

EARLY PRODUCTION

1 9 0 4 – 1 9 0 8

When actual production of Harley-Davidsons began in 1904, the fledgling firm was very much a family operation. Walter Davidson quit the railroad shop to be H-D's only full-time employee, working in a shed in the Davidson back yard, while Arthur kept his day job and helped at night, along with some part-time workers. Not only that, but early finances were eased by support from a well-to-do maternal uncle.

But one of the best early stories has to be about the badge: the Harley-Davidson Motor Company bar and shield. The Davidson boys had a maiden aunt with a talent for art, and the legend says Aunt Janet did the design, which has gone on to rank with Ford's script or McDonald's arch, along with applying gold stripes to the black paint used on those first machines. There have since been mutterings that the badge fable is just that,

The first Harley engines were based on French design. There is no mechanical linkage for the intake valve because it's opened and closed by atmospheric pressure, but these bikes do have a control allowing riders to bypass the muffler on the open road or to be quiet in town— one reason this model was nicknamed the Silent Gray Fellow.

but there's such a thing as researching a story too far, so from this soapbox, Aunt Janet gets the credit.

The first Harleys were as basic as they could be. The designers were, after all, new to the business and not even the veterans really understood just how internal combustion took place.

Harley's single-cylinder engine displaced about 25 cubic inches, making it larger than the average for the day. (The details here are vague because the builders made more running changes than they made notes.) The intake valve was above the exhaust valve, both offset from the piston, with the space between them forming most of the combustion chamber. This system, known as intake over exhaust (IOE) or pocket valve, was the conventional design of that time.

Those first singles had an automatic intake valve, meaning that the valve was pulled open when the piston went down, then pushed shut when compression began and held shut through the power and exhaust strokes, then pulled open again on the intake stroke. This system, along with the camshaft and lobe for the exhaust, did the job for as long as engine rpm was measured in the hundreds.

This early single-cylinder model is labeled 1907 and it sat in the Junaue Avenue factory's lobby for years, albeit more careful research indicates some parts might be earlier. No matter, though, because what shows here is the first use of the legendary leaking-link front suspension, and then the perhaps-surprising fact that natural rubber, as used for the tires, is white. Not long after this the tire folks discovered that adding carbon black made tires much stronger and more durable, and they've been around ever since. *Mark Mitchell/Harley-Davidson Motor Company*

Oil and gas tanks were attached to the frame above the engine, so feed was by gravity, a method still in use today for fuel tanks in all but the most exotic motorcycles.

Pioneer lubrication came to have a worse reputation than it deserved. The early engines used roller bearings, ran at low speeds, and didn't need a lot of oil, so the factory calculated the need and designed the drip feed to suit. There was also a pump for the rider to operate when the engine was putting out extra power, such as when climbing a hill. What made this look bad later was the term *total loss,* which conjured up the image of oil going to the engine, being whirled around inside the crankcase, and dumped on the ground. How it sounds isn't how it worked, but the name stuck.

The first motorcycles from the backyard shed were basic, meaning no lights or horn, a seat for operator only, one speed with some variation allowed by the belt drive, a bicycle-style coaster brake in the rear hub, no brake in front, and wheels rigidly mounted to the frame and forks.

Some of this simplicity was to keep costs down, but just as much was because the motorcycle idea was new, and the practical parts were still being developed. The carburetor was just then becoming a working instrument, for example, and the controls were intricate assemblies of levers, pivots, cranks, crevices, and rods, because the creative likes of Glenn Curtiss were just then working out the Bowdoin cable and the twist control.

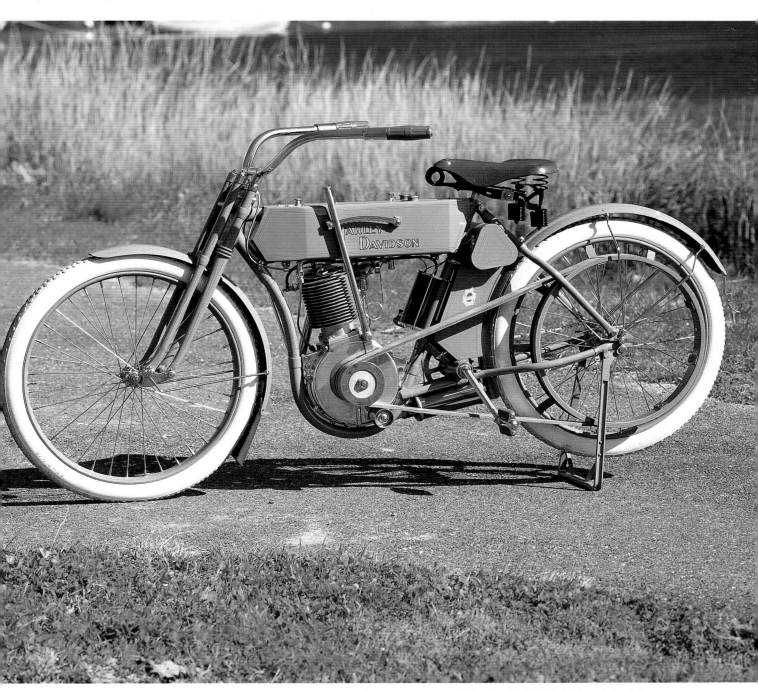

Early production Harley-Davidsons were very basic machines, as in one cylinder, one seat, and no lights. But this 1910 Model 6—so designated because 1910 was the sixth year of H-D production—has a front suspension designed by William Harley and a tensioner for its belt drive.

WALTER DAVIDSON, ENDURANCE RACER

There was another major development and another happy accident in 1908.

As it happened, William Harley was a good rider, and so was Arthur Davidson, while big brother William enjoyed the business and the convenience but never really rode much just for fun.

But Walter Davidson was, as they say in baseball, a natural.

Motorcycles, make that motor vehicles, had a lot to prove early in the century. They scared horses, ran off

Walter Davidson wore an expression of honest pride after he'd won the national enduro and put H-D into the headlines if not on the map. This is 1908, so Walter's mount has the leading-link front suspension that would be used for the next 40 years. Notice all the control rods, links, pivots, and levers it took to connect man and machine before the twist grip and Bowdoin cable were invented. You can also see that the motorcycling attire of 1908 was much different from today's. With increased speeds, a coat, tie, and cap would not be practical motorcycling gear in the modern era. *Courtesy Harley-Davidson Archives*

roads, made noise, and broke down, which was the major drawback. Not for nothing did George Hendee and Oscar Hedstrom, the powers behind Indian, invite the local press to Killer Hill so the Indian prototype could climb it with ease. This made front-page news, and Indian was famous overnight.

Because the motorcycle had something to prove, racing was as much proving ground and public display of confidence as it was sport. In 1908 the national club, the Federation of American Motorcyclists (FAM), sanctioned and organized a national championship endurance run. Endurance meant just that; the club set a nearly impossible two-day schedule, and the riders came as close as they could.

Half of the 84 entrants were out by the end of the first day. At the end of the second day, Walter Davidson had a perfect score. It was so perfectly perfect that the club gave him five bonus points for a perfect-plus finish.

The next week, Walter ran in the FAM economy run where his Model 5 single returned 188, yes, one-eight-eight miles per gallon. This was on a stock machine; stock in the sense that at that time all Harleys were assembled by hand and checked out before hitting the road.

In the long run, Walter's skill made the brand famous while his interest and enthusiasm ensured that the product would be what the motorcycle nut wanted, even before the buyer knew it for himself. Later, when H-D did form a team, Walter was in favor: Just because he didn't race for money didn't mean he objected to professionals. And he was known for being honest and generous, in an era where the fix was known and the handshake often wasn't enough.

What Harley and the Davidsons could do was make motorcycles that worked. They made and delivered two such machines in 1904 and six more in 1905. They doubled the size of the building and the crew and in 1906 produced about 50 machines, this time with a twist-grip throttle and a larger engine.

During this time, bicycle enthusiasts went racing with their motorcycles just as they'd done with the human-powered two-wheelers. While Harley-Davidson didn't have a factory team or production racer, historian Jerry Hatfield has turned up a letter, dated late 1905, in which sales manager Arthur Davidson told a prospective buyer that a Harley had covered 15 miles on a track

Pulling the lever tightens the belt; pushing eases the tension. This allowed the rider to pedal up to speed before spinning the engine and to stop the machine with the engine idling.

in Chicago in 19:02 minutes, proving that the Harley-Davidson was the fastest single-cylinder on the market.

In 1906 there came the first option, gray paint with red trim. Possibly because good manners are noticed, H-D supplied efficient mufflers, and the model was known as the Silent Gray Fellow. (Imagine how that would go over now, when even motorhomes are tagged Marauder or Predator.)

William Harley delivered his leading-link suspension for the 1907 models. To go with increased production and staff, the partnership became a corporation. Harley was appointed chief engineer, Arthur Davidson was sales manager, Walter was the firm's first president, and William Davidson quit his railroad job to become plant manager.

Seldom have there been better examples of the right people in the right place at the right time. Just as William Harley matched the profile for the best engineer, so did Arthur turn out to be a canny and effective sales manager and the right man to build a dealer network. And by the time William Davidson took over the plant, he was a foreman in the railroad shops. He was also a large and hearty man who could do the work his men were doing, and at a time when might could settle the question of right, he was big enough to do that part too.

In 1908, with the development of differences in the models, The Motor Company needed a form of identification. At first, they used a simple number system. The 1908 models were called Model 4 because they were produced during the fourth year of model production. The following year, when there was a choice between battery or magneto to power the ignition, the Model 5 had a battery and the 5A used a magneto.

Although straightforward in the beginning, H-D's identification system would get more confusing, as you will see in later chapters.

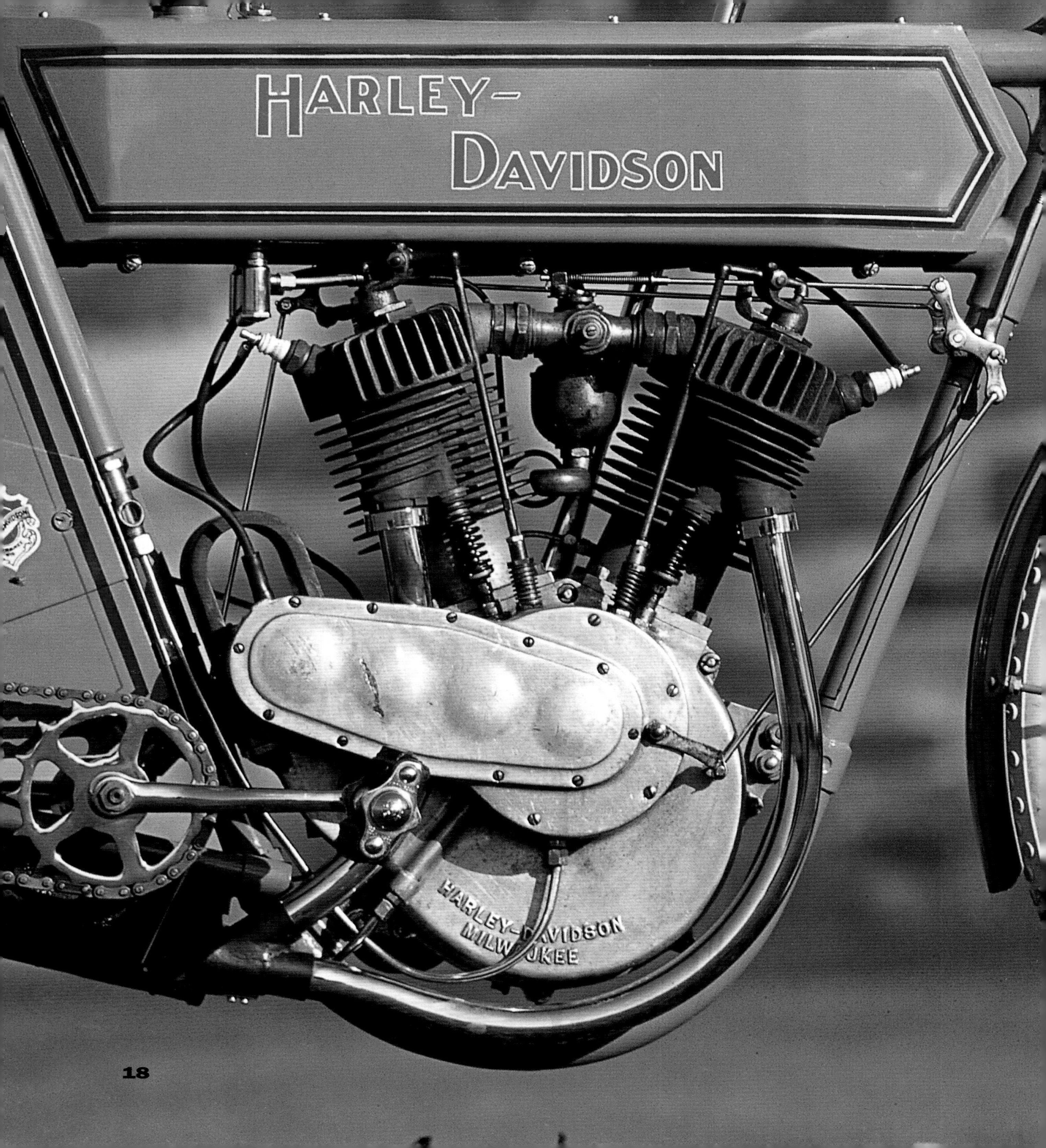
HARLEY-
DAVIDSON
HARLEY-DAVIDSON
MILWAUKEE

CHAPTER 3

V-TWINS RULE

1909 – 1929

Harley-Davidson's most enduring tradition, the narrow-angle V-twin, not only wasn't an H-D invention, but Milwaukee's version was the firm's first failure.

The idea of two cylinders set at an angle above a shared crankshaft was logical. A glance at a bicycle's conventional frame shows that once you set a single cylinder at the bottom of the frame's vee, you might as well use two cylinders, which builders began doing very early.

Researchers have found some hints of an early V-twin in the Harley archives dating back to 1907, but the first official version came in 1909, when a twin, with the cylinders fore-and-aft, inline, and with both connecting rods on the same crankpin, was added to the choice of singles with battery or magneto.

The twin lasted less than a year. The model found buyers, but what hadn't been reckoned with was that the

H-D's first successful V-twin appeared in 1911. The V-twin logic, the perfect fit of the narrow vee within the frame, is obvious here, but the real secret is that pair of pushrods—from the camshaft sited below the vee to the intake valve rockers atop the head. This made it possible for the V-twin to start via the pedals and increased engine speed.

added power, an estimated 7 brake horsepower, versus 5 for the single, was too much for the drive belt to hold, plus the twin's automatic inlet valves limited engine speed and made the engine almost impossible to start.

H-D did make progress on other fronts, however; William Harley got a patent on a two-speed rear hub, the belt control was improved, and lights became an option, either electric via generator and battery or with acetylene gas, produced by dropping pellets into a tank where the pellets dissolved in water and became a gas that was piped to the headlight and burned (if that sounds like a bother, the batteries of the day were even more so).

The big news for 1911 was the return of the V-twin, with the same displacement but with a camshaft lobe and gear for the intake valves. It was a markedly improved engine, especially now that the two-speed hub had a speed to cruise and one to climb with.

In 1912, the frame was revised to allow suspending the seat on a sliding post, which soaked up the big bumps, and in 1914 came a starting system that allowed removal of the pedals and chain, the last vestige of the bicycle ancestor. The Harley term was *step-start*, which is more elegant than *kick-start*, eh?

The next generation, roughly 1916 through 1929, saw some remarkable contrasts. We'll call this a generation because there is a constant, the use of the intake-over-exhaust (IOE) engine, the basic idea of which was seen on that first H-D engine. There were detail changes and major improvements and variations, for instance the eight-valve, fully overhead-valve racing conversions built atop the IOE cases. And there was a line of economy-model singles with side valves; cheaper to build and run.

While the major engine design was retained, there was a stream of improvements, the three-speed transmission and the foot-controlled clutch, for two. There were electric lights with battery and generator, and the stripped loss-leaders. The model line expanded until there were standard, sports, and commercial machines, along with cargo and delivery rigs.

With this expansion came the need for identification, in the plant and in dealerships. The old way, the Model 5 and 5A, didn't tell enough of the story.

By 1915 when this Model 11-J was made, the Harley V-twin came with step-start—no more pedaling down the road—a headlight, a taillight, a luggage rack, and a sliding post for the seat to absorb the worst of the bumps, and, oh, yes, the tire people had discovered that mixing white rubber with a dash of carbon black made the tires much more durable.

This 1917 V-twin introduced a major theme in motorcycle history—the cut-down. This machine, a J or JD, has a single-cam road engine, and the step-start has been shifted to the right. But notice there's no muffler or lights, and the fenders have been trimmed back. Such cut-down machines became the fashion when the factory fitted all the extras.

The new way began with letters, seemingly chosen in roughly alphabetical order: the Model E followed the Model D, with the W coming after the U and the V—except that the E was a big twin, the D had been a middleweight, and so was the W, while the U and the V were big twins.

Letters were added, also in random fashion. The basic H-D engine, the 61-cubic-inch IOE twin, was the Model J. If it came with magneto, it was the F. A J enlarged to 74 cubic inches was the JD. Late in the series, the engine got a second camshaft: the 61-cubic-inch engine was then the JH, and the 74 cubic inch the JDH. The basic engine with sports extras was the JL.

The joke now is that only two people understand Harley's system; one is retired, and the other is dead. So you can memorize the code, but you can't break it.

Factory racing was serious business. This 1921 two-cam began as a J engine, but each cylinder gets its own two-lobe camshaft, and the special frame uses the engine cases as a bridge. There's no frame tube below the engine, so the engine sits closer to the ground. No brakes, of course.

Completely different from other Harleys, the WJ Sport used a fore-and-aft twin-cylinder engine with an enclosed drive chain and girder forks. The example pictured here is an unrestored version built in 1921. The WJ Sport was quiet, efficient, and a sales flop that was dropped from the catalog after 1923.

This sounds paradoxical, but as motorcycles became more reliable and useful, motorcycling became more sport and less transportation. (To simplify, as soon as all motorcycles could get there from here, the issue became which one could get there first.)

Promoters came up with spectacles, huge, banked board ovals allowing speeds well above 100 miles per hour. They provided close, dangerous, and thrilling races, which drew the crowds and that meant everybody who picked up a newspaper on Monday knew which brand had won on Sunday.

Modest mention of private success was no longer enough, so in 1914 Harley-Davidson fielded a racing team, matching Indian and Excelsior. They raced souped and stripped J-powered specials and later had four-valve tops for the J crankcases; these were called Eight Valves because there were four for each cylinder.

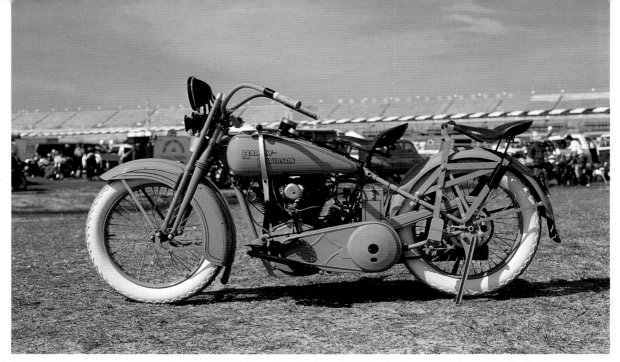

By 1927 the J-series, represented here by a 74-cubic-inch JD, used a pair of rounded fuel tanks slung over the frame tube, deeply valanced fenders for weather protection, a three-speed transmission with hand shift and foot clutch, and even a sprung seat for a passenger.

The big news for 1928 was the first use of a front brake, seen here on a JD that also has crash bars—the hoops outboard of the frame's front downtube. The left-side tank contains oil, delivered to the crankcase by working the plunger handle, just visible on top of the tank.

One of racing's recurring problems appeared now for the first time. The competition machines became faster and more specialized and less like road machines, all at once. Enthusiasts could ride to the races, but they couldn't ride and race the same motorcycle.

The board tracks were spectacular and dangerous. Make that fatal, all too often, with the victims spectators as well as riders. This was an easy target for the tabloid press—they had such even back then, before the line at the check-out counter—and professional motorcycle racing became as much show business as sport.

The benefit, perhaps the only benefit, was that the builders and tuners developed and acquired technical skill and knowledge at an accelerated rate.

Then came World War I and some canny moves by Harley's founders. The War Department (later known

Sidecars were still popular in 1928, and the JD frame came ready for the outfit to be bolted on. The black gadget below the headlight was known for years as an electrical signal, because back then if it didn't have a bell like a trumpet or trombone, it wasn't a horn. And the canister below the signal is the toolbox.

As racing got faster, the rules called for smaller engines in hopes of reducing speed, while the racers got better at getting more from less. This is an early Model B with a 21-cubic-inch single with overhead valves (OHV). It's rigged for short-track racing with no brakes, no suspension, the gear lever moved to the right so the rider has clearance to put his foot down, and a brace—the taped black thing in front of the seat that the rider wedges his right leg against. These machines were known as Pea-shooters because the engine went pop-pop-pop.

as the Department of Defense) saw the motorcycle as a useful addition and ordered thousands of examples.

At that time, Indian was the sales leader. The financial wizards who'd taken over from Hendee and Hedstrom took out the dealers, whom they saw as middlemen, and sold all the bikes they could make directly to the military.

The military used the motorcycle almost exclusively for courier and traffic control, so the actual machines were the standard road models, F- and J-series twins in Harley-Davidson's case.

Neither factory's production was reduced, except that H-D continued to supply the civilian market through its

BLACK JACK PERSHING VERSUS PANCHO VILLA: MOTORCYCLES GO TO WAR

General John J. Pershing, nicknamed "Black Jack" because he commanded African American troops early in his career, was a World War I hero and by the evidence in all the pictures, a man of military bearing and stern demeanor—Old Guard right to the ramrod-straight core. He was an unlikely pioneer, at best.

In 1916 General Francisco "Pancho" Villa, who'd been on the losing side of one of the several revolutions Mexico was having at the time, took to raiding small towns on the U.S. side of the border. Villa was a popular loser, and the Mexican authorities couldn't cope, so they gave permission for the U.S. Army to pursue Villa and his men on whichever side of the line Villa was.

Pershing led 20,000 troops into Mexico, and with the troops came motorcycles: Harley-Davidsons, Indians, and a few Excelsiors, all big twins and most fitted with sidecars.

This was the first recorded incidence of motorcycles in combat, although the police had seen the uses of two-wheeled pursuit very early in motorized history. And as it happened, this was nearly the only time motorcycles were used in actual combat.

Pershing's men were free to experiment, and they fitted the sidecars with machine guns. The rigs made a good platform, and the timing, when compared to the time it took to haul a machine gun and cart with mules and then rig it for fighting, was in the cycle's favor.

Perhaps the best part of the story is that Villa's soldiers also had motorcycles, and there's a surviving snapshot of Pancho himself, grinning like motorcycle nuts always have, about to leap on an Indian's kick-start pedal. If you are one of those novelists who mingle fact with fiction, next time have Black Jack and Pancho motocrossing across Sonora, Indian versus Harley.

In real life, this never happened. What happened was the armies learned that motorcycles were faster than mules and horses but that riding and shooting at the same time wasn't like sitting on a horse and slashing infantry with a sword. So as Villa managed to elude Pershing's larger force, the military learned motorcycles were better used for courier duty than as motorized cavalry.

But Harley-Davidson took advantage of photo opportunities and showed the public lots of shots of Harleys in the army. What the record doesn't show is Black Jack on a Harley; while his troops piloted cycles of various makes, there's no evidence he ever rode one himself.

normal outlets, so when the war was over and people had cash, time, and a taste for adventure, Harley had a dealer network, and Indian didn't. Harley took the sales lead and kept it until Indian went out of production 35 years later.

During the 1920s H-D concentrated on the J-series twins, with some smaller singles for commercial buyers and some experiments such as the W-series Sport, a fore-and-aft twin smaller than the Js. It was quieter, easier to start and ride—but not enough people wanted a practical motorcycle, and it didn't look right. The model was dropped, and it took H-D management a long time to try any other radical notions.

CHAPTER 4

SIDEVALVE SURVIVORS

1928 – 1935

This may be an unheralded virtue, but something must be said in favor of the person who can openly and cheerfully adopt an idea not invented here.

That's pretty much what William Harley and the Davidsons did in 1928.

The intake-over-exhaust (IOE) engines did a good job through the 1920s. The singles had become twins; the twins grew and developed. There was a special run of high-performance J engines (the 500-series), and the J lower end was used for the four-valve racers.

It was all to the good, except that Indian had gone to sidevalve engines, flatheads as they said then, and the sidevalve Indians were as powerful as the IOE Harleys, plus they made less noise, needed less maintenance, and cost less to make.

William Harley and the engineering staff knew this and designed new engines. They considered overhead

The V engines had four single-lobe camshafts in the gearcase (as H-D-speak terms it) in the right-side engine case half. Each lobe opened one valve, which was complicated but precise. The heat shield on the rear exhaust pipe of this 1934 VLD, the sporting 74, is a later addition.

valves, which were being used on English motorcycles and by U.S. car makers, Chevrolet notably, but OHV engines are more complex and cost more to make. So H-D took the practical approach, looking at the amount of performance needed, and made the largest, least-expensive engine that would deliver the goods.

To this practical approach, Harley-Davidson added its own principle, which is to not make all the moves at the same time. So while the J-series twin continued in production, along with the singles and the competition machines in 1928, H-D introduced a new line of middleweights, powered by 45-cubic-inch sidevalve V-twins. The new model was designated D. It had a front brake, which H-D also added to the J-series that year, along with a four-tube exhaust and dual headlights. The D's engine joined the gearbox via the primary drive. It had four one-lobe camshafts in an arc below the valves, and its generator was mounted vertically at the engine's left front, parallel to the front cylinder.

Because of its configuration, Indian fans called the new machine the three-cylinder Harley. The D received so much abuse because it was a direct competitor of the Indian Scout, also a 45-cubic-inch sidevalve V-twin. By no coincidence, H-D and Indian had tried smaller V-twins, the Sport and the original Scout, respectively, and learned that the large and powerful middleweights sell better than small and thrifty ones.

For the 1930 model year, the D was retained and the J-series 61s and 74s were replaced by the V-series, 74-cubic-inch sidevalves that came with different stages of tune but in the same displacement.

Harley-Davidson's teapot had acquired its very own tempest.

H-D's introduction of the sidevalve engine came as quite a shock. For generations Harley fans had argued with Indian fans over the merits of the intake over exhaust versus the sidevalve, and Pow! one day H-D took the Indian path. Some Harley folks felt abandoned and proclaimed the J engine to be the best motorcycle engine ever made, and 60 years later you can still find some vintage owners who'll tell you exactly that.

No one could dispute the fact that both the D-series and V-series bikes had serious flaws when they first went into production. Revisions were made to the engine and frame, and the factory organized what amounted to a recall campaign long before such things were common. All the troubles, though, were worth the effort. The big sidevalve

The all-new 1930 V series looked more familiar, with its paint scheme and dual headlights carried over from the 1929 J-series. But the sidevalve, 74-cubic-inch engine and three-speed transmission (plus reverse in case you fitted a factory-backed sidecar, as seen here) shared no parts.

1930 HARLEY-DAVIDSON 45 cu.in. RACER
MOTOR NUMBER 30 DLD 5621

BUILT IN 1932 BY: *Harry Stailer Sr.*
H-D DEALER SINCE 1905, HOU? TX

RIDDEN BY: *Bill Anderson* #8 HOU., TX
1932-1940: WON TEXAS STATE T.T.
CHAMPIONSHIP 1934; POCHILO RANCH COURSE,
WACO, TEXAS, AGAINST 80 cu. in. MACHINES

1937 GALVESTON, TEXAS, BEACH TIME TRIALS
SET 45 cu. in. TIME AT 98 PLUS M.P.H.

BOUGHT BY: *Ricky Rouse* BEAUMONT, TX IN 1940
WHO ENJOYED MANY WINS. RICKY JOINED
THE AIR FORCE 1941. LEFT BIKE WITH
Woody Leone Sr. #0 WHO RODE IT BEFORE & AFTER
WORLD WAR II WITH GOOD RESULTS
RICKY RETURNED; RODE & RETIRED IT IN 1947.
THE BIKE SUFFERED SERIOUS DAMAGE IN TWO
FLOODS AND WENT AS JUNK TO AUSTRALIA.
IN 1990, WOODY LOCATED AND BOUGHT
IT BACK FOR $3,750. HAND MADE MAGNESIUM
PISTONS AND MANY OTHER PARTS NOT AVAILABLE
2,000 HOURS

Racing was saved during the depths of the Great Depression by motorcycles such as this 1930 DLD—the *D* representing the 45-cubic-inch sidevalve V-twin that ushered in the H-D Flathead era, with *DL* standing for sports tune. Seen here as restored in 1992, this DLD was raced in TT events, a pre-motocross off-road contest. It's been stripped of lights and mufflers, and the front fender has been moved to the rear while the rear fender has been thrown away.

By 1933 the V-series, represented here by a VL, the standard customer model, had acquired its own look, with more graceful tanks and fenders and some extraordinary paint schemes. The sidevalve, 74-cubic-inch engine and gearbox are separate, each mounted on the frame and joined by a primary chain and housing.

The VL's rocker clutch pedal is just above the floorboard, while the hand shifter is located by a gate on the fuel tank. The springer forks don't have shock absorption yet, so the knobs on the sliders outboard of the fork springs are tensioned to keep the bounces under control.

engines were reliable. In 1930 H-D sold the plain V, the VL (the most popular version, which had a higher compression ratio), and the VM or VLM, the only difference in the latter being the magneto ignition. (Even then there were those who didn't trust motorcycle batteries.)

The V models were about 100 pounds heavier than the Js had been. They also were lower and had more power. Performance was close to equal with the JDH, except that a VL could hold top speed longer. The V and D were contemporary as well, with foot clutch, hand shift, and three speeds. For the 1932 model year reverse was added, mostly for the benefit of sidecar operators. However, the major news in 1932—aside from the collapse of the world's economy—was that the 45's generator was remounted, horizontally this time, and the frame was reworked, changing the model designation from D to R.

These were tough times, as the Great Depression got worse, and some extreme measures were taken.

Several years earlier, H-D had offered single-cylinder models, either sidevalve or overhead valve (OHV). They were offered at home and sent overseas, where practical machines were more in demand, especially when Harley-Davidson was a major exporter.

The models didn't sell and the singles were dropped from the catalog, but in 1932, when any sale was a plus, the company hauled out the parts for the models they hadn't sold or serviced, and reverse-shipped, brought back stocks from overseas, and reintroduced the single, with a 21-cubic-inch sidevalve engine called the Model B (yup, same as the much-more-famous 1932 Ford). At $195 it was the cheapest

The Model D with its vertical generator, was mocked as the "three-cylinder" Harley-Davidson. The Indian people love to tease.

The styling of the D was essentially identical to the Model V. Check the generator side and you'll know right away.

Harley-Davidson ever, and something close to 1,000 were assembled and presumably sold. Not much help, but surely better than letting the parts rust away.

The economic depression also led to the collapse of professional racing. Harley-Davidson was losing money, Indian was living day-to-day, and Excelsior had quit the motorcycle business. No one could afford to buy or race the specialized and exotic 500-cc machines that had been contesting the national events.

In an attempt to keep motorcycle racing alive in 1934, the American Motorcyclist Association, backed by Harley and Indian, drew up plans to make racing affordable. The

The 45-cubic-inch R series, which replaced the D models in 1932, got a new frame, with room for the generator to be horizontal at the front of the cases. The R machines—such as this 1934 RL—were junior big twins, so to speak, and could be bought with options including the fringed buddy seat, luggage rack, case guards, and brilliant paint schemes.

Looks can deceive. For 70 years, 1929 through 1999, Harley's big twins used two tank halves fitted to look like one tank. The left side of this 1934 VLD holds gas and oil, the latter delivered by the plunger pump aft of the gas cap. And yes, there are two keys, one for lights, the other for the ignition.

JOE PETRALI, CHAMPION RACER

Joe Petrali was a racer who set a record that not only will stand for all time but shows just how out-of-balance and unsporting racing had become in the depths of the Depression.

In the 1935 season, Joe Petrali won every national championship race. Every one.

To some degree this happened because in 1935 there was one factory with a racing team, Harley-Davidson, and that team consisted of one man, Joe Petrali.

These facts, however, don't give Petrali his due.

Joe Petrali, H-D's lone pro racer, set a national speed record aboard this Knucklehead-powered streamliner in 1937; however, this picture tells a story that's not quite accurate. First, the bodywork wasn't as slick or as stable as it appeared to be, so Petrali made the actual speed run, 136.183 miles per hour, on Daytona's beach with the bike bare. Next, the air cleaner on the left doesn't mean that the photo is flopped; it means there was a second carb for the Model E. And the generator has been replaced by a magneto. The tanks and the tail section are done up in Art Deco, just like the production bikes, because H-D wanted the public to get the impression that the record-setter was a lot more stock than it was. *Courtesy Harley-Davidson Archives*

He was a total professional. Born in San Francisco, Petrali began hanging around motorcycle shops at a very young age and assembled his first machine, an antique Indian single, when he was 13.

Petrali was such a good racer he got sponsorship from Indian, and when that firm dropped its team, Petrali was immediately hired by H-D. He was under contract, racing only, and kept his day job with Albert Crocker, an Indian dealer who later infuriated Harley-Davidson by building a 61-cubic-inch OHV motorcycle that was faster than Harley's equivalent. Petrali's allegiance was to racing, first and foremost. Back when he was racing Indians, he showed up at the track and discovered that his Indian had been lost in transit. As it turns out, a Harley guy had a bike that wouldn't run, so Petrali fixed it and rode to victory.

Petrali won hillclimbs on H-D's limited-edition, which was based on the D engine with overhead valves, and he won on the dirt and the board tracks with the 21- and 30-cubic-inch singles, known as "Peashooters" because of their exhaust notes.

In 1937 Petrali rode a modified Model E, the Knucklehead (see chapter 5), to a new national speed record of 136.183 miles per hour, at Daytona Beach. The photos show a streamlined tail section and fairing. In fact, the streamlining made the bike unstable so Petrali stripped the bodywork and muscled his way to the record.

Then came the new class, Class C, with big bikes and a different style, and Petrali didn't like them, or they didn't like him. So he went elsewhere, and when Howard Hughes defied the government and lifted the giant eight-engined Hercules (it wasn't made of spruce, and it wasn't named the Spruce Goose, except in the tabloids, but that's another legend for another time) into the air, the only other man in the airplane was the flight engineer, Joe Petrali.

A major factor in H-D's survival through the 1930s was police business. This 1934 VLD was first sold to a police department and fitted with a fire extinguisher as well as a siren and red light.

The OHV Model E was supposed to go into production for 1935, but it wasn't ready. The dealers needed something new, so H-D developed an 80-cubic-inch option for the sidevalve 74s, and the model carried over—witness this 1936 VLH—in case the Model E didn't make it.

professional classes had been called Class A and B, so the new class was called Class C, and the machine's owners, using production machines, would compete in it.

Because the most sporting production bikes were the 45-cubic-inch Harley Model R and the Indian Scout, 45 cubic inches was declared the eligible engine size, with sidevalves required. Some imports competed as well. One dealer in particular, Reggie Pink, sold Triumphs, Nortons, and other English bikes from his shop in the Bronx. He was an AMA member and a racer, so to be sure his customers could race, Class C was also open to 30-cubic-inch (better known as 500-cc) singles with overhead valves, which were the sporting English machines of the day. This was a bold move that worked. A generation of new stars, riders who wanted to race but couldn't buy a racing machine, appeared on the track, and brought their friends, and racing was revived, perhaps even improved.

CHAPTER 5

SPORT SAVES THE DAY

1936–1947

As the slogan goes, when the going got tough, Harley-Davidson got going. The tough part was, of course, the Great Depression, which hit the motorcycle business and the sport of racing especially hard. At that time a motorcycle was, for the most part, an option, an easily deferrable purchase, which most people did. H-D and Indian soldiered into the 1930s, however, keeping their corporate heads above water and depending on sales to police departments and other government agencies.

The H-D founders knew motorcycles, so early in these bad times, when they were cutting their own salaries and putting workers on part time, they authorized a new model, one that would be so new and exciting and sporting that the H-D fan would simply have to have one.

Discussions and preliminary planning began in 1931, but because the engineering department was small and busy and there wasn't money to invest, the actual debut of the new machine, scheduled for 1935, was delayed until the 1936 model year.

The new bike, designated Model E and nicknamed Knucklehead, was worth the wait and the investment, evidenced by the fact that it would become the basis for Harleys in production 65 years later.

Not that the Model E was radical, because it wasn't. The engine was a 45-degree V-twin, with cylinders fore and aft and fork-and-blade connecting rods, just like the 1911 Harley V-twin. But the Knucklehead was an overhead valve (OHV) which gave the 61-cubic-inch engine more power than the H-D (or rival Indian) 74- or 80-cubic-inch sidevalve engines. (Harley had of course built OHV engines before, in single-cylinder street models and 45-cubic-inch hillclimbers, but until 1936, the extra cost hadn't been worth the return in sales.)

The E used a dual-stage oil pump, delivering oil from the tank to the engine and then scavenging the oil and sending it back to the tank—again, not radical; in fact, Indian had gone that route several years earlier. It was the modern way and a better way. The Model E also had a stronger and lower frame, and although the rear

The OHV 61 fills the frame's vee perfectly. The knuckles of the nickname are actually nuts for the rocker shafts atop the heads. One camshaft with four lobes was a departure from previous H-D practice. The device at right front, with the chromed cap, is the ignition timer.

The 1936 Knucklehead, formally the Model E, revived Harley-Davidson's fortunes and the motorcycle market, set the style for generations to come, and was the ancestor of the F-series engines of model year 2000.

wheel was solidly mounted, the clutch was operated by foot and the four-speed gearbox by hand.

This new model had what it took. It looked modern; it looked new; it looked right. And it sold. H-D's founders had been correct. Initial teething problems were quickly overcome. The Knucklehead was the fastest motor vehicle the buying public was likely to own or encounter, even capturing the national speed record in 1937.

The Motor Company then began playing from strength. The 45s (the R-series) were given recirculating oil systems, dry sump as we'd say now, and renamed the W-series. Because the 45s were the sport bikes, they were offered in a high-performance series, the W, WD, WDL, and WDLR. In 1941, Harley offered the WR— a stripped-for-racing version right off the showroom floor with no lights or brakes to unbolt. That model and the archrival Indian Sport Scout were the backbone of American racing for the next 10 years.

In terms of line and balance and distinctive looks, the Knucklehead was as good a motorcycle design as has ever been made.

By no accident whatsoever, the air-cooled Model E engine bore a strong resemblance to the air-cooled radial aircraft engines of the period. The container behind the engine is the oil tank, and the box behind that holds the tools.

The 45-cubic-inch middleweights followed the styling trends of the larger models but were renamed the W-series when they gained recirculating oil systems. (Hint for bike spotters: The middleweights from D through R and W and X have the final drive on the machine's right, while the larger models have the drive on the left.)

The 1939 WLDD, seen here at the vintage races in 1993, was the factory's high-performance model and came with special aluminum cylinder heads. It's rigged here for road racing and still has its brakes as well as a pad for riders when they are scooted back off the seat for lower wind resistance.

In 1937, the sidevalve twins were enlarged to 80 cubic inches and relettered U and UL, while the 61-cubic-inch E was joined by 74-cubic-inch versions, designated F and FL in 1941.

Then came the war. The United States, of course, entered World War II late in 1941, following the Pearl Harbor attack on December 7. But there were foresighted people in government and industry, so H-D, Indian, and the War Department had actually begun research for military motorcycles back in the mid-1930s.

H-D designed and built an experimental motorcycle patterned on the opposed-twin BMW, which was

This 1943 EL has the optional fat front wheel and tire, which was supposed to give a softer ride, and the round air cleaner fitted to the later Knucklehead engines, along with the instruments mounted on top of the fuel tanks and the fender trim. All these reappeared 50 years after this motorcycle was new.

H.D. M/C MEDIU

previous spread

The army's motorcycle, the WLA, got raised suspension, extra clearance between fenders and tires so mud couldn't jam the wheels, a giant air cleaner, and a scabbard for a submachine gun. Although the motorcycle corps didn't see much combat, their cycles provided a valuable service as scouts and couriers.

By itself on a stand, the Knucklehead shows us where the name came from, with its polished nuts retaining the shafts for the rocker arms. The four-lobe camshaft is located where the pushrods intersect. The chromed cap to the right of the front pushrods is the ignition timer, which houses the points and condenser. The generator mounts at the front of the cases and is driven by a train of gears from the right-side flywheel. *Courtesy Harley-Davidson Archives*

This is a field meet and in some ways a parade as well. It is 1939, and the members of the Yonkers (New York) Motorcycle Club are dressed in semimilitary garb, which was popular before World War II put everybody in uniform; they are doing a precision drill at the Fishkill Gypsy Tour. In this era, clubs belonging to the AMA would often ride to a resort or park for a weekend of fun, games, and fellowship. *Courtesy Harley-Davidson Archives*

used effectively by the German Army, while Indian offered a cross-mount V-twin that their principal stockholder and CEO, Paul duPont, himself an inventor and engineer, had thought up.

The Allied forces used these motorcycles for scouting and courier duty, and H-D and Indian served the war effort by supplying tens of thousands of mildly modified sidevalve 45s, called, in Harley's case, the WLA—WL for the normal 45, A for the army version.

What Harley-Davidson had, in effect, was a series of niches. The W-series was for sport and competition; the E and F were the road burners and prestige models. Clark Gable had a Knucklehead, for instance, while the U and UL sidevalves hauled sidecars and did commercial

Pictured are the Milwaukee fairgrounds in 1947; the rider is Leo Anthony. You would suppose the machine to be a WR, the production racer. But no, not quite. That's a WR engine, all right, with a front end complete with an empty brake drum. But notice the double downtubes of the frame, the clutch lever on the left bar, and the shift lever in front of Anthony's boot. Ah ha! Now we know, 50 years later, that 5 years before the K and KR came out, the racing department was experimenting with stiffer frames, foot shift, and hand clutch. *Courtesy Harley-Davidson Archives*

DOT ROBINSON, RACER

Like most genuine heroines, Dot Robinson didn't set out to right wrongs or set the world straight. She just didn't see why gender should limit sport, so she didn't let it happen.

Many believe that women discovered motorcycles about the time they discovered the Feminist movement. Not so. As soon as the motorcycle appeared, there were women riding. They toured and raced and rode cross-country even back in the teens. There weren't that many female riders, but, nevertheless, women have always been part of the sport.

In Dot Robinson's case, her family's involvement in the motorcycle industry piqued her interest. Her family (the Gouldings) made sidecars for the big Harley twins. And through her motorcycle connections, Dot met and married Earl Robinson. He saw Dot at her family's shop and bought parts until she would date him.

It simply wouldn't have occurred to Dot Robinson that she shouldn't ride motorcycles, or that it was something ladies didn't do, so she did it. Dot and Earl became an impressive motorcycling team. This was in the 1930s, when only hard-core motorcyclists were riding and when the American highway system was just coming into being. The machines were markedly better than they'd been in pioneer days, so cross-country records were literally made to be broken, and

they were. In 1935 Dot and Earl set a New York–Los Angeles record in a Harley big twin fitted with a Goulding sidecar. Their time was 86 hours, 55 minutes, for the 3,000-plus miles.

Dot also rode enduros as a hobby, and legend has it that some people objected to girls getting all muddy, and there was talk of banning women. She heard the rumors, so, leaving Earl to mind the store, Dot rode cross-country on a mission. Face-to-face with each member of the AMA competition committee, she asked, "Are you going to try to stop me from competing?" And face-to-face, no man had the nerve to say anything beyond, "Gosh, no."

And that was that.

But the incident seems to have raised her consciousness, so in 1940 Dot and some other women created the Motor Maids, a feature of rallies and field meets for the next 20-plus years.

The Motor Maids had two main rules: One, membership was limited to women who rode their own, their husband's, or their father's motorcycles; and two, any member caught trailering her bike to an event was expelled from the club.

Dot rode her pink GLH well into the 1980s, always with good manners albeit, we suspect, we know what would have happened if she'd been challenged to a race. The Motor Maids are still a part of the sport, although now they're not quite so tough on the trailer queens.

This photo was taken in the 1940s, surely in the parking lot at H-D's Juneau Avenue headquarters. When this photo was first pried from the archives, the official word was that the bike was a road-racer made for Europe. Not so, mostly because the engine here looks to be a version of the DAH, a limited-production 750-cc (45-cubic-inch) OHV V-twin made for and used by the factory's hillclimbers in the late 1920s. Also, there was no 750 road-race class in Europe, and anyway, the Europeans had made importing motorcycles all but illegal. Not only that, the rider is dressed for the road, and the bike has a toolbox (the canister atop the front fender) and wears a rear stand. This machine was definitely made for highway use. Why did H-D develop this bike? Because early in the 1930s, before the Knucklehead was finalized, H-D's founders were thinking about a production OHV 45, like, oh, the Excelsior Super X, and this machine surely was an experiment in that direction, if not a prototype. *Courtesy Harley-Davidson Archives*

work. And there was also the Servi-car, the three-wheeler towed by repair shops and used by police departments for parking meter enforcement.

H-D management has always had its corporate eyes open. For example, there were several prototype OHV 45s built before the founders decided that a true performance model had to be at least a 61. And the educated eye can scan the files and see hand clutches on racing bikes 10 years before they appeared on road machines. In keeping with this, even while busy with military work H-D knew the war would end, and that when it did, civilian demand would be stronger than ever.

However, they decided, first, to keep the existing models coming—no need to spend money on new stuff when the buyers will spring for the old, after all. At the same time, management wanted to enlarge the motorcycle market, which led in 1947 to the introduction of a single,

a 125-cc two-stroke based on a German (DKW) design, the rights to which H-D collected as part of its war effort.

Most of this plan worked out fine. The buyers were happy to collect the 45-, 74-, or 80-cubic-inch versions of the prewar machines, which gave H-D time to design and phase in the updates they knew were needed. At the same time, it's fair to say that this is when Harleys began to be seen as outmoded, which in many ways they were. Equally, we know the punchlines, that the upcoming new models would expand the factory's lineup, that the big bikes would create a market of their own, and beyond that, all the modern rivals would come to copy in the 1980s the looks that were outmoded in the 1940s.

CHAPTER 6

THE LITTLE ENGINES THAT DIDN'T

1947–1976

Harley-Davidson's single-cylinder models were, as Herbert Hoover said about Prohibition, "An experiment noble in purpose." The singles were, for the most part, good motorcycles, and so was the motivation behind the program. However, just as there is no thing stronger than an idea whose time has come, so is there no surer failure than the good idea whose timing is wrong.

The thinking was correct, surely. H-D's owners, along with the folks at Indian and those overseas, figured there would be a demand for motorcycles when World War II ended, and they hoped to attract new enthusiasts as well as the experienced crowd.

H-D engineers had no experience with little bikes. The beginner market had been dead for 15 years, after all. But at war's end Harley got the U.S. rights to use the German manufacturer DKW's design, saving a lot of time and expense.

A very different Harley-Davidson, the 125-cc two-stroke single introduced in 1947, was a direct copy of the prewar DKW. Note the girder forks, hand clutch, foot shift, and left-side kick-start.

The new model was a very basic motorcycle, as the DKW had been an inexpensive youth machine. Introduced in 1947 as a 1948 model and called either the M-125 or the S-125, the single displaced 125 cc produced around 3 brake horsepower, topped out at 55 miles per hour with the rider trailing his or her feet to reduce air drag, carried one person, weighed maybe 200 pounds, and had a wheelbase of 50 inches. Front suspension was a girder fork; the rear wheel was rigidly mounted in the frame, just like the big twins, but the 125 had a foot shift and hand clutch, a first for production Harleys.

H-D would later upgrade it, adding a telescopic fork and an engine enlarged to 165 cc; it was called the Hummer, and most of the little bikes are known by that name today.

One can't fault the factory for trying. H-D was willing to do what the market wanted—they offered the Pacer and the Scat; off-road singles and dual sport models; even several scooters, including one named Topper; and a couple of tiny bikes.

But still the machines didn't sell. Why? First, and the major factor, as it turned out, the public wasn't all that eager to ride motorcycles. And people who were interested often didn't like the old-boy atmosphere at the Harley store, while the old boys themselves, the dealers, weren't used to having young people in the place and didn't enjoy having to teach new buyers how to stay upright on the way home.

But while H-D struggled, it did not make the fatal mistake Indian did. In the late 1940s, Indian bet the farm on introducing the public to motorcycles. They advertised in the mass media, using movie stars such as Roy Rogers for spokespersons to sell their neat, small machines. These efforts failed, and it was clear at the time that Harley's *not* having tried to expand the market was why H-D was there and Indian was gone.

In the late 1950s, another company, Honda, had better luck with small machines. They advertised in the mass media as well, offering neat, small, and reliable (which the

The 1948 S-125, later nicknamed the Hummer, was small and basic but complete, even though they had to mount the horn outboard of the drive chain, behind the engine. And we'll see that tiny fuel tank again.

The Sprint had style. This is a 1964 in dual-sport trim with a high front fender, exhaust pipe, and even a case guard below the engine. It's Italian red, of course, and has a teardrop tank too shapely not to share.

The Sprint H was the sports version, but even so it came with a dual seat and full road gear. The box with the label contains the battery.

Indians weren't) motorcycles. Their slogan was "You Meet the Nicest People on a Honda," and this time the public went for it. The good idea had found its time.

H-D couldn't compete with Honda on a dollar-for-value basis, not with exchange rates and wages being what they were, nor could the company, still privately held, afford to build new designs. What they could do was buy a distressed Italian company, Aermacchi (which loosely translates into Airmachine) and import that maker's 250- and 350-cc four-stroke singles, calling them Harley-Davidson Sprint.

They were good little bikes, attractive and modern. The lovely teardrop tank, seen later on the touring

DICK O'BRIEN, RACING COACH

When we talk about a racing team, we often forget that racing is half the equation, and the other half is the team. And for a team, you need a coach.

No stick-and-ball squad ever had a coach more, well, more coachlike, than Dick O'Brien, who was head of the Harley racing team and department for many years. O'Brien began as a kid swapping work for parts, then as a racer of cars and motorcycles who realized that what he built went faster than he could ride it.

He joined The Motor Company as racing engineer in 1957. It was at this time that the sports bike, the Sportster, switched to overhead valves, while the racing bike, the KR, kept the sidevalves because H-D didn't have (or wouldn't spend) the money to make a road-legal 500-cc single to compete with the imports. H-D's flatheads remained competitive, thanks to being 750 cc, but it was really O'Brien's work that kept them equal. He was an engineer and worked out in the shop with the guys, honing and experimenting, and every year picked up a brake horsepower or two, until by 1968–1969, their last years, the KRs were producing 65 brake horsepower from 45 cubic inches.

But that is the mechanical side of the story.

The other side of the story reveals that O'Brien had a knack for getting the most out of those he worked with. He was a gruff bear with a deep, raspy voice that's just right for dressing down guilty parties. He cajoled and blustered and persuaded and almost always knew when to do which. He hired talent and fired talent when it got uppity. He played the press like a violin, handing out secrets when it served the team's interest, clamming up when it didn't. He bolstered morale when it sagged and played tuners and riders against each other when rivalry made the rivals work harder.

Harley-Davidson has long had mandatory retirement, but nobody who saw "O.B." in action ever doubted that he stayed on the job well past the limit, because there wasn't anybody in H-D's head office brave enough to tell him to leave before he was ready, which he was in 1985.

Sportsters and early Superglides, came from the sporting version of the Sprint and was too good to not use over and over. But, again, the public didn't go for them. The Sprints came in touring, sporting, dirt, or racing form. They were squeezed into streamliners and set records at Bonneville. They were the basis for the factory's short-track and 250-class road-racing efforts, and the public could buy kits to build or convert racing machines for privateer efforts.

Still they didn't sell. It's true, the little Italian machines needed more care and understanding than the big twins did, and the young crowd buying small singles was more apt to abuse and neglect them than the old guys were, but even so, part of the problem was that the Sprints weren't native Harley-Davidsons, so to speak, and the other part of the problem was that in sheer technical terms they weren't up to Japanese standards or even up to date.

That came next. Two-stroke engines had taken over in off-road, as in enduros and motocross, so Harley-Davidson switched too and had Aermacchi

Sprints became a mainstay of amateur competition and were even used in professional short-track events. This is the 350-cc model, an ERS, with the production engine fitted to a lightweight frame, available through the factory.

make a line of two-stroke singles, in dual sport (road legal), enduro, and motocross forms. The factory sponsored a full team in motocross and even innovated, making rear suspensions that looked like the sliders and stanchion tubes that were used for the by-then-worldwide telescopic forks in front.

By the 1970s, Harley-Davidson was in trouble. H-D had limited resources. There'd been the expansion into small motorcycles and scooters and golf carts, which weren't selling, and there were the traditional twins, the Sportsters, Superglide, and FLHs, which were selling.

In short, Harley-Davidson went back out of the small motorcycle market. Sold them all, on the floor and off, even threw in a trailer if you'd buy the bike.

The sad part is obvious, in that the little Harleys were good motorcycles and the effort failed through no fault of their own.

The unfair part is that the critics have long yammered about how Harley-Davidson has kept on cranking out those air-cooled, pushrod-operated overhead-valve (OHV) twins when the world has gone elsewhere, while in fact and as this record shows, H-D has made a valiant effort to meet the public's demands: it's the fickle public that's the culprit here.

The good side to the story is that despite failing to make a dent in the small motorcycle market, H-D weathered the storms and remains financially strong. It may even be safe to bet that we'll see the Harley range broaden in the near future, and that the single will return.

CHAPTER 7

THE BIG TWIN ERA

1948 – 1980

Radical tradition, when applied to Harley-Davidson, isn't the contradiction it would be elsewhere. In 1948, having satisfied the demand for just about anything with an engine, Harley-Davidson made a major change to big twins.

The E and F models, with 61- and 74-cubic–inch engines, respectively, got new cylinder heads. They were made of aluminum, and they used hydraulic valve lifters—this at a time when Detroit still relied on iron components. The new heads used a rocker cover that looked (if you used your imagination) like a cake pan, leading the fans to call the new models Panheads.

Just as soon as the new top end proved itself, the rest of the motorcycle was brought up to date, step by step. (H-D's leaders knew they could offer the old stuff when the market allowed, and knew to improve when improvement was demanded.)

Thirty years after the Knucklehead, the Panhead was replaced by this top end, known as the Shovelhead. The three engines were different in detail but shared a basic structure and many components.

In 1949 the leading-link forks, which dated back to 1907, were replaced with telescopic front suspension. The model designation remained F or FL, but the factory coined the name Hydra Glide. In 1958 the rigidly mounted rear wheel was given suspension: conventional shock absorbers and swingarm, and the still-FL was named the Duo Glide. In between, as it were, hand clutch and foot shift became an option for the big twins, beginning in 1952, although for several model years the old hand shift and foot clutch were listed as standard and the newly swapped controls were supposedly an option, even though all but the hard-core few went with the new (and better) way.

Thus, the Knucklehead and early Panhead were built in 74- and 61-cubic-inch form, while the factory first phased out the sidevalve big twins and then the 61 overhead-valve (OHV) Panhead. The 61 had been a low-stress model and was replaced by a mild version of the FL. At the same time, the factory offered a 74 with polished intake ports and camshaft timing, and it claimed a 10 percent boost in power. Its designation was FLH, the H representing an improvement, as seen with the J and JH (the H does not stand for Highway or Hot).

Along with the smaller models detailed elsewhere, Harley-Davidson began experimenting with diversification and became interested in plastics and fiberglass. This led in turn to the use of the new materials for saddlebags.

The FL and FLH were offered with plastic or fiberglass saddlebags, along with larger fuel tanks and windshields.

Perhaps the major leap into modern times came in 1965, when the Panhead, named the Duo Glide after rear suspension was offered in 1958, got electric start and became the Electra Glide. This conquered a

Why it's called the Panhead is obvious; less obvious is that this 1948 FL still has the springer forks, rigid rear wheel, and hand shift inherited from the Knucklehead.

Where the Hydra Glide gets its name is equally obvious. Telescopic forks were new for this 1949 Panhead, along with a right-side chromed hub cover to mimic the front brake on the left.

Rear suspension brought the name Duo Glide. This 1959 FLH also has a hand clutch and foot shift—the rocker above the left-side floorboard. And that spring-thing above the rocker? That's a helper spring for the clutch, which was designed for foot power. The helper's imaginative nickname is Mousetrap.

major obstacle (even though many Harley folks had looked on the electric leg unfavorably since 1914, when Indian offered electric start only to withdraw the option because the batteries of 1914 weren't up to the job). While kick-starting a big motorcycle is wonderfully satisfying when it works, it's shamefully frustrating when the engine doesn't respond. Not only

that, the Japanese had made electric start standard and cheap and effective, making the other manufacturers appear behind the times.

As soon as the electric start worked, the factory took another major step, for 1966, with new cylinder heads—the Shovelhead. It was so called because the rocker boxes look, if you use your imagination, like

The improved Panhead engine justified electric starting, which arrived in 1965 with the Electra Glide. The kick-start is still there (as the early electric starters did give trouble), while the massive battery literally displaced the toolbox.

the business end of a coal shovel. The new heads used improved flow and higher compression and raised the power again, while being cleaner and quieter in operation than the Panhead had been. As you can see by the following numbers, the added power wasn't so much noticed as it was needed.

According to historian Jerry Hatfield, the early 1940s FL with springer forks weighed 550 pounds, presumably dry but fully equipped. The 1964 FL, weighed by *Cycle World* with half a load of fuel, topped out at 690 pounds, while the electric starter and bigger battery added at least 75 pounds. And *Cycle World*'s test 1967 FLH weighed in at 783 pounds. Thus, the 60-brake-horsepower FLH option wasn't too much power, not compared with a 515-pound Panhead rated at 48 brake horsepower.

The big Harley was no longer the performance king. Instead, quoting from the factory's brochure for the optional package of saddlebags, top box, and fairing, the FLH was King of the Highway, defining if not inventing the touring motorcycle.

Fashion, of course, demands change, so when some Harley riders began adding bags, boxes, case guards, fairings, lights, fringe, and so forth, other Harley riders began taking things off.

At first they mimicked the TT racers, adding raised suspension and exhaust and small tanks to their big twins; then they went beyond function, with high pipes, extended forks, and no front brake or fender. The creations were called choppers, and they mostly were for show.

But then Willie G. Davidson, who, like his grandfather's partner, had gone off to get an engineering degree and came back to the family firm, saw an opportunity. The design staff took an FL frame and engine, installed the lighter XL front suspension and light, and

The King of the Highway package was touring equipment, as seen on this 1966 FLH wearing a windshield and fiberglass boxes on the rear fender. This example has front and rear case guards, dual exhausts, and every chromed cover known to the accessory division.

Here's a Harley that never was. When the English and Japanese triples and fours eclipsed the Sportster as a performance bike, the engineers at Juneau Avenue considered answering in kind producing this mock-up of an overhead cam, 750-cc V-twin with a 50-degree included angle. It has Sportster bars, lights, and fenders, an XR-750 fuel tank, and an XR-based frame. But budget constraints overruled the project, so the larger (and cheaper to build) XL-1000 carried on. This machine went directly from the drawing board to the history book.
Courtesy Harley-Davidson Archives

THE AMF ERA

By the end of the 1960s, Harley-Davidson's founders had died and the company had gone public but didn't have the working capital to take advantage of the motorcycling boom caused by the arrival of Honda and others. So, early in 1969, Harley-Davidson was acquired by American Machine and Foundry, better known as AMF, a conglomerate working on the notion that leisure industries were a good place to be and on the notion that motorcycles are a leisure industry.

By unhappy chance, the takeover came at the same time as a boom in sport and off-road motorcycles and at a time of change and disquiet across the cultural span.

H-D wasn't prepared for motocross, the Honda 750, the Triumph triple, or the Kawasaki 900. The federal government had begun imposing rules, such as requiring that all gearshifts had to be on the right with neutral between first and second, not to mention emissions regulations. And all of this came at a time when H-D was embroiled in labor troubles, resulting in serious problems for The Motor Company.

Some thought AMF had bought H-D so they could lose money doing a poor job making inferior motorcycles. It's true that AMF management didn't understand motorcycling and made some poor decisions. Most likely H-D survived only because of a loyal dealer and owner network. But because AMF did spend lots of money on the plant (versus spending it on the product or the people), the AMF ownership ultimately kept H-D in business and set the stage for success down the road.

You can't have a silver lining unless you begin with a cloud.

The Superglide made its first appearance in 1971. It created a lot of news and attention because the Superglide didn't look like anything H-D had ever produced.

Outrageous, eh? The original Wide Glide was totally chopper as you can tell by the flared rear fender, raked forks, high bars, and flamed tank. And this was the last time step-start was offered on a production H-D. *Courtesy Harley-Davidson Archives*

added a fiberglass seat and rear fender, which was first seen as a seldom-ordered option for the Sportster.

The experiment was shown in public in the late 1960s, with the factory's involvement not mentioned. The reaction was favorable, and in 1971, the FX, named for the F-series engine and X-series parts, was introduced as the Superglide. It was a big hit, once the press and the public got used to the idea of a production chopper. And later, when the big tanks were swapped for the lovely teardrop tank from the Sprint and when electric start was standard, the Superglide sold.

Partly through intuition and partly by taking the right notes, the people in charge of H-D had set the styles for what was to come.

CHAPTER 8

HIGH-PERFORMANCE RETURNS

1952 – 1985

While Harley-Davidson's post–World War II plan was to continue production on the big bikes and make radical moves with the lightweight models, they ended up developing a line of sporting middleweights. H-D was pushed in this direction by a buying public that was enamored with British bikes, especially the 500-cc and 650-cc twins.

H-D's first move in 1952 was to replace the W-series (the sidevalve 45s) with a new model line that was more different than it looked.

The series name was K. The new bikes still had a 45-degree V-twin engine with valves on the side of the bore, and its 45 cubic inches translated into 750 cc. But the K differed in that it used unit construction, with the transmission a cluster of gears on shafts tucked into a cavity in the rear of the engine cases,

instead of having an actual gearbox bolted to the back of the engine.

And the K had telescopic forks and a swingarm rear suspension, with four speeds forward, foot shift, and hand clutch, fully as modern as anything from England, Italy, or Germany.

Included in the K-series was the basic, street-going Model K, the mildly souped-up KK, and the race-only KR, a highly tuned engine in a racing-spec frame; both the KK and KR were much more different from the road version than they looked, plus you could buy a swingarm and shock absorbers to bolt onto the KR frame and add brakes, a big fuel tank, and later a streamline fairing to make a KRTT. There was also a desert racer, basically a KR engine in a K frame, called the KRM.

While the K had looks and specifications, it lacked power. So in 1954 the engine was given a longer stroke, increasing displacement to 883 cc, and it was relettered the KH. H-D also made a tuned version, the rare KHK, and the even more rare KHR and KHRTT, the purposes of which can be guessed by the letters.

The profile of the K engine, with its narrow-vee center carb and arc of four one-lobe camshafts below the valves, is still an H-D trademark 50 years later. The shift lever was on the right, like the British rivals and unlike the bigger Harleys.

The 1952 Model K, with telescopic forks, rear swingarm, and unit construction engine and transmission, was about as all-new as any Harley since the WJ Sport of 1919.

The KR and KRTT were a match for the imports at the races but sales were lackluster at best, so in 1957 H-D took the last step to conventional wisdom, introduced an overhead-valve (OHV) engine for the sporting crowd, and invented the mass-produced Superbike. The name was Sportster, surely as good a name for a motorcycle as has ever been thought up, equal to, oh, Thunderbird or Black Lightning.

The designation was XL. Odd, in a Harley-Davidson sense, because the X was a repeat: a World War II–era machine done for the military but never produced as a civilian bike was designated XA, with the A for Army. Plus, H-D had until then used one letter, as in J, E, or W, for the basic model. The in-house guess has always been that there was a plain X at one

The seldom-seen KHK was a K with a larger and more highly tuned engine. It sold by the handful, perhaps because the lack of visible differences subtracted from the brag potential.

The KR was all racer, with highly modified internals behind the K profile and with a special frame that could mount either a rigid section for dirt-track racing, as seen here, or a swingarm with shocks for TT or road races. And yes, the fuel tank came from the little 125-cc Hummer.

The first XL, the 1957 Sportster, mimicked the look of the K-series, except that the OHV engine was a lot more different from the K or KH than it looked. And the XL's big fuel tank and headlight nacelle made it a little brother to the FL series.

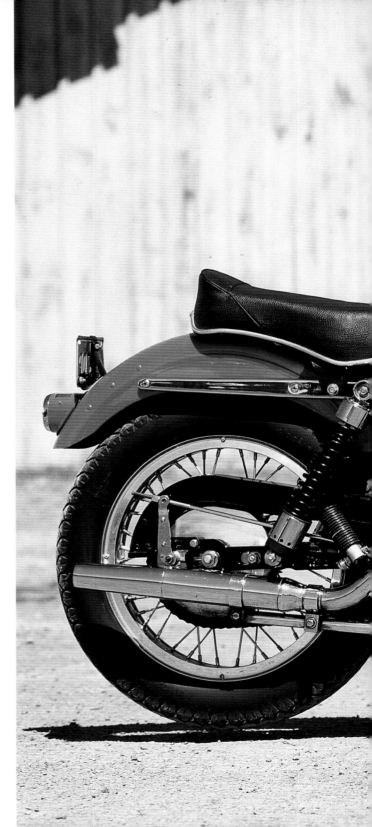

time, but the tuned version, as in JD or FL, worked so well the X was never produced. That's a guess.

More important here, most of the XL was just like the KH, as in suspension, unit construction, and so forth. The XL engine displaced 883 cc, again like the KH, but the XL had overhead valves, a higher compression ratio, bigger bore and shorter stroke, all of which meant more power and performance.

The Sportster was an instant success—mostly because the factory listened to the market. The first XL was almost a junior FLH, but when the dealers asked for speed and sport, the factory offered the XLC, a stripped XL for desert racing in California, and the XLR, a mix of XL and KR parts, and they topped the mix with the XLCH, an instant classic with a tuned engine, a "peanut" fuel tank from the KR (which took it from the little Hummer), low, dual exhausts, low bars, and a solo seat.

There is a lot of history captured here, as the XLCH had a tuned XL engine fitted with two single exhaust pipes, the magneto ignition, and the ex-Hummer fuel tank used first by the KR. This was also the origin of the hamcan air cleaner and the little eyebrow mount for the headlight, both still in production.

This is a factory publicity shot, posed to introduce the XLCH in 1959. The studio has gone to lots of trouble propping the bike in an attack mode, but nobody bothered to have the guy change into riding gear rather than slacks and shoes. Never mind, what is most significant now is that this is the first use of that eyebrow headlight mount and small light, and of the small peanut fuel tank the XLCH got from the KR, which in turn borrowed it from the Hummer. *Courtesy Harley-Davidson Archives*

The XLCH was the original mass-produced Superbike, more than a match for the imports. One reason H-D went to using 883 cc on the label rather than 54 cubic inches was because the imports were 650s and then 750s. As we all know, bigger is better.

In 1968, there was a divergence in the series. The XLH was offered with electric start, while the XLCH still had kick-start only. And then the competition came out with triples and fours and even bigger twins, which meant that the Sportster no longer ruled the street.

The factory countered with a larger 1,000-cc version, which had options such as a larger fuel tank, a thicker seat, and a fiberglass seat and rear fender (nicknamed boattail). H-D even tried for a vaguely racer

In its final form, the 1968–69 Lowboy seen here, the KR-TT was highly specialized and still effective, in that it won the Daytona 200 both years, against much newer rivals. The KR-TT had its own frame, Italian brakes and front suspension, full bodywork developed in the wind tunnel, and a ferociously tuned version of that sidevalve K engine. The 1968 team bikes were the first to use the Team Harley orange and black paint.

look called the XLCR, CR standing for Café Racer, an English fad at one time. The XLCR didn't sell, which of course made it instantly collectible.

The XL line was also the basis for a lot of competition involvement, as the drag racers discovered it was easier to make the XL engine bigger than it was to keep the FL engine together. The second actual XL model was the XLR, a stripped-and-souped mixture of the XL and KR used for national TTs, where for some obscure reason there was still an Open class. By the late 1960s, however, the XL proper lost its performance mantle to the two-strokes, triples, and fours and became more practical and useful at the same time with lots of options, including big tanks and windshields.

The Sportster was adapted to the changing times, which were changing at great speed. In 1981, a group of H-D managers, members of the founding families, and so execs brought in by AMF put up all the money they had or could borrow and bought The Motor Company from the corporation.

The slogan was "The Eagle Flies Alone." The fact was, the eagle was burdened by the need to service a tremendous debt. As one way to increase sales and get

continued on page 79

CALVIN RAYBORN AND THE KR

Realists, or perhaps the cynics, like to say there's no such thing as luck in racing, and it's true, the winner is most often the person who's stayed up latest and worked the hardest.

Plus, there is talent—and when there's mention of talent, you have to include Calvin Rayborn.

He was a shagger, zooming around San Diego on whatever motorcycle he could find, dropping off blueprints and legal papers. Then he went to the races and came to the attention of Len Andres, the San Diego H-D dealer who'd tuned son Brad to the national title in 1955.

Andres began building bikes for Rayborn, and Rayborn turned out to be a natural talent, arguably the best of his era. In 1968, after the KRTT wore orange and black for the first time, and the factory team filled Daytona's first two rows, Rayborn not only won the 200, he lapped the field.

In 1969, the two-strokes were there, and the KRTTs were slower than they'd been the previous year. Yamahas got the pole and 7 of the first 10 places, while the Harleys were 10 miles per hour off the pace. And then, on race day, it rained. The 200 was postponed for a week, so team guru Dick O'Brien had time to find out why the KRs had slowed down, and it turned out to be the new dual carbs, which were fixed.

When the racing finally resumed, the fastest Yamaha's ignition fell off, the fastest Suzuki threw its rider off—and Cal Rayborn won again, riding a KRTT that was, to quote *Cycle*, "definitely not the fastest thing around."

It was the KR's last hurrah, and finest hour, and best of luck.

The XLCH Café Racer was a good try that didn't work. It was a mix of a stock XL-1000 engine, an improved frame derived from the XR-750, some XR styling hints, a bikini fairing, and black paint. The public wasn't interested in blending dirt track with European profiler, and the XLCR didn't sell.

The XR-750 began winning dirt track races in 1972, and the team guys say they'll win with XRs in 2000. An XR is a specialized, highly evolved racer, but this one, which was raced by pro contender Jason Fletcher, still displays that K-model profile and the ex-Hummer, now peanut, fuel tank.

XR-750, TIMELESS RACING MACHINE

Back in 1934, when the factories and the dealers and the AMA set out to save racing, they agreed on the equivalency formula, 750-cc sidevalve versus 500-cc OHV. It worked well for 35 years, but by 1969 the imports weren't selling many 500-cc models and Harley's venerable KR was the only sidevalve left. The AMA, with heavy pressure from the importers, came up with new rules, allowing any 750-cc engine produced in quantity and sold to the public.

H-D's overnight answer, when the team was short of money and time, was a destroked version of the XLR, named the XR-750 and based on the iron-top XL engine. The iron XRs were lovely to look at, but their engines blew up early and often.

In 1972, having taken the time, been given the money, and learned the lesson, the race team built the alloy XR-750, with better material, shorter stroke, bigger bore, more power, and longer life.

The XR-750 was the machine for dirt track—miles, half-miles, and TT, while the XRTT, a different frame with the same two-carb engine and an efficient fairing (based on the late KRTT glass) ran the road courses.

The four-stroke twin couldn't compete on pavement with the fours or the two-strokes, however, so by 1975 H-D was out of road racing. But the narrow-angle V-twin is still the best on dirt, and at the turn of the century, Harley's XR-750, in all the basics just as it was in 1972, is still the best in the class.

While most XR-750s can be found turning left and spitting roost on the flat tracks of America, a select few have been converted for street use. Who is up for feet-up broadsides onto Main Street?

The XR-1000 combined elements of the XR-750—the two-carb heads and dual exhausts—and the peanut fuel tank and the XLX-style solo seat. The price was high, the reliability low, and the sales dismal.

The Evolution Sportster has been a top seller since its 1986 introduction, and it's now offered as a sport, a custom, or even a racer.

Continued from page 74

some ink, in 1983 H-D introduced the XLX, a barebones, loss-leader Sportster with a solo seat, black-only paint, low bars, no extras, and a sticker price of $3,995. The bikes sold as fast as they could be made, while the campaign that came with the model helped turn the corner, as Harleys became, after some years of disfavor, the bike to buy.

With two such steps forward, there had to be one step back. And there was. Also for 1983, the factory tried to cash in on the success of the race-winning XR-750 and mixed that machine's two-carb heads, alloy top end, and high dual exhaust pipes with the XLX trim and peanut tank.

The model name was XR-1000. It didn't offer all that much performance and the sticker price was $7,000, so sales were dismal. Worse, the few who did buy discovered the engine was fragile, so much so that the factory had a new run of engine cases done at the foundry. Perhaps worst, the XR-1000 didn't look all that different, which meant H-D was sort of selling a Ferrari in a Fiat suit.

But wait, there are two bright spots here. One, because the public wasn't sold, the collectors swept in and kept the prices up. Two, while the XLX sold and won new buyers for Harley, it was a loss leader, but because the price for the XR-1000 was so high, sources in the factory say each one sold at profit.

So even when it lost, the Lone Eagle won.

CHAPTER 9

INDEPENDENCE AND EVOLUTION

1980 – 1997

While the grudge many Harley lovers have against the American Machine and Foundry has died extremely hard, AMF did at least one favorable thing during its ownership—they authorized the engineering and investment of the FLT.

The timing was nearly perfect. In 1980, Harley-Davidson unveiled the new FLT model. It had the F-series engine, enlarged to 80 cubic inches but in a new frame and with a frame-mounted fairing instead of the batwing barmount fairing used by the now-classic FLH. More important, the FLT engine and transmission were isolated from the riders by shock-absorbent mounts (the mounts are often called rubber, but strictly speaking, they are made of a different material).

The FLT was big—and it worked, in essence redefining the touring motorcycle and putting H-D in the news as well as selling.

The V2 (Evolution) engine was nearly new, but its ancestry can easily be confirmed by comparing it with the Knucklehead portrait in chapter 5. *Courtesy Harley-Davidson Archives*

Soon after, some members of the Davidson family, some old-line H-D guys, and some executives who'd come to H-D from AMF, bought H-D from AMF, putting up all the money they had and mortgaging their futures to make up the difference. This was a win-win move. AMF wanted to get out of the leisure business, and Harley's new owners thought the corporate atmosphere soaked up too much time and energy.

With the new ownership in place, H-D continued to innovate. And, while the AMF managers hadn't been bikers, gearheads, or party animals, they'd authorized the engineering and investment for, first, the FLT.

In 1981, H-D introduced the FXR. It had the same isolation-mount principle as the FLT, but in another new, much lighter frame. The FXR came in sport and touring versions, the former generally acclaimed as the best Harley ever made, the latter an excellent bike but too conventional. Import riders didn't want a Harley; Harley buyers didn't want to look like the imports.

The original plan was that the FXR would replace the original FX line and be called the Superglide II. This didn't happen. Instead, while developing improvements such as a five-speed transmission for the big twins and a

81

The FXB Sturgis was named for the South Dakota rally, and the black-with-polished-alloy theme was radical. But the real difference was the final drive, with a notched belt and pulleys replacing the chain for the first time in nearly 50 years.

Next came the Evolution, the V2 engine, seen here in a custom-painted 1985 FXR. The V2 engine was traditional in broad specs and in outline, but it was virtually trouble-free, while the FXR handled like a sports bike and looked as new as it was.

The Heritage Softail defines nostalgia. Not only does this 1991 example look as if it has the rigid rear wheel of its ancestors, the owner has added a toolbox and a horn with a bell, and once again, you can get just about any paint scheme you can imagine.

belt final drive for the Harley twins, the engineers had been working on something even bigger—a new engine. Well, it was new in the sense that almost all of the parts were new, as well as improved, but at the same time the V2 engine, quickly nicknamed "Blockhead" by *Cycle World,* was an 80-cubic-inch, 45-degree, air-cooled, two-valve, four-stroke, single-camshaft engine. In other words, it had generally the same specs as the Shovelhead, the Panhead, and the Knucklehead.

The Blockhead, now generally known as the Evo, was phased into the big twin line, phased because meanwhile, Harley's guys had been to a show and seen an outsider's notion of building a rear suspension; it was tucked beneath the frame rails and made the bike look

CHARLEY THOMPSON, THE PERFECT PRESIDENT

There are no blueprints for creating top executives, but if there were, Charley Thompson would have been the perfect pattern for H-D—except perhaps that Thompson had a misspent childhood and didn't ride a motorcycle until he was in his thirties.

When he did take that first fateful ride, he was a high-school teacher and football coach, but he liked motorcycling so much he became a Harley dealer. He was so good at that, he became H-D's national sales manager. And he was so good at that, he became H-D's president when H-D was reclaimed from AMF.

In his dealership days, Thompson used intuition and his own experience to formulate a basic piece of wisdom: The most important thing a dealer can offer is something for the customers to do on their bikes. Thus, as president he instituted the quality control program, giving the workers the chance to do good work and to take pride in their work, leading in turn to a product the customers could trust and take pride in.

That done, in 1982 he climbed aboard a stock FLT with a sealed engine so there'd be no tricks and rode it, flawlessly, from the Pacific Coast to Daytona Beach. He died in 1988, and those who knew Charley still miss him.

This 1992 Ultra Classic FLT is called a dresser because it has extra lights along with a sound system and every chrome extra in the catalog.

like the old rigid-rear motorcycles. H-D licensed the idea, and it became, for the 1984 model year, the Softail. (For the record, the in-crowd bikers called the old-time, rigid-rear bikes Hardtails.)

This was a tremendously successful move. The original Superglides evolved into a model line, with different paint, larger (21-inch instead of 19-inch) front wheels, and a belt drive. The Softails were in 1984 what the Superglide had been in 1971, the hot ticket. And just as the Superglide demanded dues in the form of kick-start, so did the Softail scorn the isolation mounts of the FLT and FXR. The Evo engine bolted directly to the FXST's frame because, in the spirit of William Harley, real motorcycles vibrate and real motorcyclists want it that way!

And William Harley, the man who designed the leading-link forks of 1907, had his design brought back in 1988 on the Softail—leading-link forks. While markedly improved and refined, the Springer was essentially the same concept that first appeared decades earlier.

The bar-mount fairing returned on the FLHT because some buyers didn't like the frame-mount fairing of the FLT. As these three bikes demonstrate, however, it's the same frame, full touring rig, and V2 engine on either model.

H-D's newest model line is the Dyna Glide, which replaced the FXR. This is a 1995 FXD. The framework bolted to the fender brace behind the rear shock is a mount for luggage, meaning this is an FXD Convertible, with touring gear that can be mounted or removed in minutes.

The Road King, seen here in 1996 model trim, was an FLT minus extras including fairing, top box, and sound system, saving weight and money.

The Heritage Springer was new for 1997 and used the big front wheel and tire with the revived leading-link forks, making this model a combination of two popular trends. The blue-dot turn signal lenses, backrest, and duffel bag are extras.

The tradition of evolution, making one change and seeing how it works, then making another change, had become The Motor Company's motto.

For 1986 the Sportster XLX kept the designation but got a new engine, the Evolution XL, with the same bore, stroke, and displacement (883 cc) as the original 1957 XL. But the new engine shared only a few parts with the original; it was all alloy instead of having cast-iron heads and barrels. Next, the 883 grew into an 1,100 and then a 1,200; bikes with the optional dual seats and big tanks became models of their own, and there was even the Hugger, a lowered XLH that was intended for women, not that H-D ever admitted this.

The Evolution era was a revolution, in the sense that the new mechanical bits were so much better than what they replaced. They attracted buyers who wouldn't have gone inside an old-time Harley store. Some dealers won't even work on anything made before 1984.

More important in this era was that H-D went public, sold stock, and got out of hock, becoming a financial fairy tale praised round the world. Harley-Davidson became a business legend not because of technical advances, but because H-D could, first, read the public pulse and second, fill a lot of niches with not a lot of parts. It was kind of like having Ford, Ferrari, and Honda under one roof.

The Sportster became the best-selling motorcycle model in the United States—not the best big bike, but the best-seller period. The FLT and FLHT (the one with the batwing fairing) were the class of the touring class. And the XR-750 ruled the national championship.

Everyone who was someone had a Harley. Even celebrities were shown in the tabloids careening around on Softail Heritages, wearing I-Got-Attitude T-shirts.

All this from what amounted to variations on two engines and four or so frames, mixed, matched, juggled, swapped, and disguised.

87

CHAPTER 10

NEW AND IMPROVED

1 9 9 4 – 2 0 0 0

Harley-Davidson swept into the 1990s on a roll, selling all the motorcycles they could make and enlarging the factories so they could make more. Much of this success can be attributed to H-D's attention to details that were important to buyers. During the early and middle part of the decade, the focus was on fine-tuning. The changing of a few cosmetic details allowed H-D to offer many different models without too much hassle.

One example of this can be seen with the FLHT. The buying public liked the FLHT with the batwing fairing better than the original rubber-mount FLT, so the FLT was dropped from the line at the end of 1996, and then returned to production in 1998 with a shorter screen and was called the Road Glide. The FLT's basic frame and engine, meanwhile, had been offered with a windshield and called the sport option, but when it became popular in 1994—it was the lightest and, therefore, the most nimble of the T-series—it

The new Twin-Cam 88 motor is a modern interpretation of an early 20th century design.

was renamed the Road King. And, of course, there was the Electra Glide. You really do need a catalog to keep track of the players.

Another attempt on H-D's part to appeal to the buyers involved the FXR-series. This series had been phased out in favor of the Dyna Glides, to the dismay of the more sports-oriented Harley crowd. And then, in 1998, the FXR returned. Briefly. There were 900 FXR2s and 900 FXR3s made (and snapped up.) The factory reproduced the frames, fitted V2 engines, and did half the run, the R2, with a 21-inch front wheel and slotted rear wheel, and the other half, the R3, with 19-inch front and a flamed fuel tank.

Factory spokespersons said they didn't discover 1,800 leftover FXR frames in a barn; they instead wanted to test H-D's ability to produce special runs of special models, so that's what they did. They also claimed to have no plans to build any more FXRs.

In addition to all the fine-tuning, in 1998 Harley-Davidson introduced another engine, a bigger twin, and like its predecessors, it was as much new as it was improved. Its name is the Twin Cam 88. Note that the big twin went from E to F when it grew from 61 to 74

The Night Train was a 1999 Softail with black crackle paint, forward controls—that's the rear brake lever way up there in front of the exhaust pipe—and the V2 single-cam engine.

cubic inches but kept the F designation when it became the 80 and then the 88.

The Twin Cam 88 has, no surprise, two camshafts, one for each cylinder, with a straighter and less variable path from camshaft lobe to rocker arm. And the engine displaces 88 cubic inches, thanks to a shorter stroke and much larger bore, but it's still a 45-degree V-twin, is air-cooled, and has its cylinders directly aligned fore and aft.

So, although the Twin Cam shares only 18 parts with the V2, it's still another descendant of the 1936 Model E. And while the five-speed gearbox is techni-cally a separate component, the mounting of engine to primary to gearbox is so rigid as to make the Twin Cam a unit design in everything except name.

Starting in 1998, the Twin Cam engine was phased into production, using fuel injection for the topline FL touring models and a carburetor for the Dyna fitted with the new powerplant.

The Evo big twin remained in production for two more model years, in the Softails; the factory said this was because Softail buyers liked the traditional shakes and rattles.

continued on page 94

The 1999 Road King, seen here with windshield detached, came with the twin-cam 88 engine; the quick way to spot the new engine is the oval air cleaner.

SPORTSTERS FOREVER

Somehow, until now, there's been no mention of the Harley-Davidson official motto: If It Ain't Broke, Don't Fix It.

The motto's evidence is the Sportster, still the XL-series, still 883 or 1,200 cc, still four one-lobe cams, still with air cooling. Just about every part had been changed since its 1957 introduction, but the specs are the same, and sales are higher than ever for its several versions—the Sport, the Custom, and the lowered Hugger. There is even an AMA-series for XLs stripped and raced on dirt tracks and road courses, just like the original Class C races of 1938.

The Sportster is still the Sportster, which must rank it right alongside the Ford Model T and VW's original Beetle in terms of living long and prospering.

ERIC BUELL, ENTREPRENEUR

In 1983, Eric Buell, an engineer and racer, left Harley-Davidson and formed his own motorcycle company. Buell had the rights to a racing-only 750-cc two-stroke and went into business just in time for the 750 race-engine class to be abandoned. So he bought up Harley's supply of XR-1000 engines, in surplus at the home plant, and began building race and semirace machines with radical, lightweight frames, full streamlining, and Harley power.

What entrepreneurs do best is move fast and take chances. Buell did both, and each time he brought out another model it was better and more useful and sold in larger numbers. There were teething problems, but Buell buyers, like Harley owners in the past, so liked the good days that they ignored the bad days, until Buell had the money and expertise to produce usable sports bikes, different and fast, using modified XL engines.

Harley-Davidson noticed this. And the managers knew they had a problem of their own. A large share of the H-D market was based on nostalgia and fad—being the first guy on the block to have a new Harley that looked like an old Harley.

So in 1997, Harley-Davidson bought majority control of Buell, giving him the capital and technical backing needed to produce inventive, daring, and legal motorcycles.

Early Buells were race-oriented, fully enclosed, and about as graceful as this RR-1000, powered by the XR-1000 engine, looks. They didn't win races, and they didn't sell.

Current Buells, for instance this 1999 X1 Lightning, are lighter, faster, more agile, and do win races. Power comes from a modified Evo XL engine, and only a sports bike could get away with the huge and efficient air cleaner and muffler.

The VR-1000 has only a trace of H-D heritage: It's a 60-degree V-twin and water-cooled. At the end of six years of competing in the AMA Superbike series, the VR's best finish has been second, twice.

Model year 2000 brought the FDXD, the sports Dyna, with dual front brakes, cast wheels, several shades of black, and an artful disguise of the balance tube joining the exhaust just behind the gearbox.

Continued from page 90

They were putting us on, because for the 2000 model year the Softails got the Twin Cam Beta engine, as the factory called it, a twin cam 88 except that the cases had been enlarged to fit a pair of counter-rotating balancers. The original rubber-mounts and then the Twin Cam Alpha, so to speak, didn't cure the vibrations. They isolated the riders from them. But the Beta engine cured the shakes, a truly amazing and impressive feat of engineering.

The cloud that accompanies this 1990s silver lining popped up in 1994, in the form of a road-racing program featuring a different sort of Harley-Davidson— the VR-1000. It's as different a machine as anything

New for the model year 2000 was the Deuce—(a play on numbers and words both), a Softail with the counter-balanced beta version of the Twin Cam 88 engine and a new, conservative sense of style.

seen at Juneau Avenue (the company's corporate head-quarters in Milwaukee) since that WJ Sport of 1919.

The VR-1000 is a 1,000-cc, racing-only Super-bike, although H-D fudged the rules by declaring the model a production bike, getting it certified by the Polish government! It uses overhead cams, water cool-ing, and is a V-twin with a 60-degree included angle.

None of the other racing teams have objected to its questionable certification, because the VR-1000, after five years, is still hopelessly slow. It's never won a race; it's

never even come close despite the team hiring top riders for the kind of money you'd expect to pay a top guy who's about to spend a season being blown into the weeds.

The Motor Company has backed this project because the owners and managers believe in the future. When the next wave breaks, when Harley-Davidson needs to match Honda, Triumph, and BMW, motorcy-cle against motorcycle, when nostalgia isn't as good as it used to be, Harley-Davidson will have the plant and the people and the products they're surely gonna need.

INDEX